In memory of Erin Smith —

You Got This!

Erin
2

TIME
TRIALS

Eric Smith

WESTBOW
PRESS®
A DIVISION OF THOMAS NELSON
& ZONDERVAN

WestBow Press books may be ordered through booksellers or by contacting:

WestBow Press
A Division of Thomas Nelson & Zondervan
1663 Liberty Drive
Bloomington, IN 47403
www.westbowpress.com
1 (866) 928-1240

ISBN: 978-1-5127-4281-7 (sc)
ISBN: 978-1-5127-4282-4 (hc)
ISBN: 978-1-5127-4280-0 (e)

Library of Congress Control Number: 2016908209

Print information available on the last page.

WestBow Press rev. date: 6/13/2016

CONTENTS

And we know that in all things God works for the good of those who love Him, who[a] have been called according to His purpose.
—Romans 8:28, NIV

CHAPTER 1

WHY?

Sixteen-year-old Wes Strong timed his jump perfectly, so that the screwdriver thrown at his legs just glanced off his grass-stained tennis shoe.

"No wonder you can't play football at the high school. Can't even start a stupid lawnmower," were the words thrown at him by his father with at least as much force as the screwdriver if not more. He had gotten used to the sting of things thrown at his legs in anger, but he never got used to the venom of the words. Bruises heal quicker than words he had learned early. He had decided a long time ago that whoever said, "Words will never hurt me," obviously didn't know his father.

"I knew that was coming," Wes muttered as the stubborn lawnmower finally roared to life after his father tinkered with it for a few minutes. Ever since he decided not to play football after the previous freshman season, Wes knew that pronouncement would eventually come from his father. Not that football ability translated into small-engine-repair expertise. His father just needed the right amount of beer and anger to unleash his verbal assault on his son.

I just don't get it, he thought as he went about his weekly three-hour ritual of cutting the grass and then raking the clippings as his father watched from his chair on the back porch with a beer in his hand. *What did I do to him besides being born? I do everything he says. Stay out of trouble. Don't smoke. Almost straight As. Go to church with Mom. Sure don't see him there. Why is he always mad about something? And it's usually at me.*

His lips quit moving, but the barrage of thoughts kept coming as he spiraled downward yet again into a seemingly bottomless well of anger, frustration, and despair. The sweat poured out of his body in the hot July sun, not in a healing balm, but in rivulets of hurt rising higher and higher brought on by his father's constant verbal attacks.

***

Last year, he told me to find a job or he would put me to work full-time around the house in the summer. Rode my bike all over town looking, looking, looking. Finally found a part-time job at the drugstore. What did he say? "I'm not driving you all the way to the other side of town to work. Buy yourself a car." It wasn't like he was letting me drive anyway. Had my license a year, and he never let me drive his car except a few times with him in there. So to be able to get to work, I bought the crummy VW for three hundred dollars with the money I made cutting grass. And then he wonders why I have never dated. Everybody else is a year ahead of me now. What do I know about dating? "They want it as bad as you do" was his great motivational speech. World-class advice there for sure.

What does he care about me playing sports either? He never comes. "No use to come if you're not going to play," he says. So, I tried lifting weights in the off-season after the ninth grade to get stronger for football. He wasn't about to come pick me up from that either. "Get a ride or walk," he said. The only one who lived close by was one of the assistant coaches, but I never knew till I got to the weight room if he could give me a ride. Then, it would take a couple of hours to walk the six miles home if I couldn't get a lift. It sure was embarrassing that time our preacher stopped and gave me a ride after I had walked about halfway. Reverend Frank just had to come in to say hello and see what was going on. There was my father passed out on the couch. That was all my fault too for making him look bad. That was the end of weightlifting.

And all those threats to "cut me off." Do what he says or "I'll cut you off." What is he going to do—kick me out, not feed me? I don't know. I'll definitely pay for my own college one way or another with a loan or something when the time comes. Sure don't want to owe him for that. Who knows what he is capable of doing? All I know is the way he used to grit his teeth together when he spanked me or was screaming at me or Mom, I thought they would crumble or he was going to explode. I'll never forget the way he could grit his teeth in anger and move his lips cussing nonstop. It was almost like a ventriloquist, but not funny at all. I wish it had been just a spanking. He'd beat the daylight out of my legs with his belt. So much anger. I ought to be a world-class jumper by now—the way I tried to dodge the licks. I wish I knew what those were for and where all that anger comes from. I'm not even sure I should have been born. I don't know. Maybe I do deserve it.

I know one thing for sure. Mom sure doesn't deserve the way he treats her. If I had a nickel for every time I've heard him cuss her, I'd be a rich man. I guess he thinks I don't hear him screaming at her at night after I've gone to bed. All those nights of squeezing my hands together in prayer till my fingers were numb, begging God to make it stop. I must not be doing that right either because it sure hasn't helped. Things he's thrown in anger—vases, dishes, pictures of Grandmom. Cords cut to the TV or her sewing machine as some sort of punishment. I guess he "cut her off." I remember the time when I was little and Mom and I were watching *Rudolph* at Christmastime, and he came in there, pulled the cord on the TV, and cut the wire right in front of us. Just because he was mad about something, and I guess we needed to be punished. No matter that it was Christmas and I was crying. Nice Christmas memory. Why is it always at Christmas too?

I know he has hit her. I haven't seen it, but it sure has sounded like it sometimes. The few times I've gotten out of my bed when he was yelling to try to get him to stop, he screamed at me to get back in there right away or I'd be next. I'd search her face the next day for physical evidence. Last fall, when I finally earned a letter playing JV football and she was going to buy me a letter sweater to put my letter on was a real downer. I was kind of excited to finally have achieved something in sports. As we were looking in the store, trying to pick one out, I noticed she had heavy lipstick on. After getting a better look without her knowing I was staring, it was obvious she was covering up a bruised lip. And all I was thinking about was getting my "letter sweater." How selfish. I'm thinking of a stupid sweater while she goes through no telling what. Kind of took the fun out of it. Who knows what she goes through that I know nothing about?

I love my mom, but I have no idea why she stays with him. Actually, I have two ideas. One, she is a nurses' aide, so how could she support us alone? And, more importantly to her, you don't divorce, especially not in the South. And especially not in the small town of Walhalla, South Carolina, where everybody knows everybody. You marry for life—no matter what. As a devout Christian woman, she couldn't do that. I guess her religion makes it easier for her. At least he lets us go to church on Sunday. But no other times. The few times she has tried to go back for other activities, he tells her not to come back. "I can get some black lady to clean the house," he says.

I don't understand what he has against religion either. I've never seen him go to church except for a few funerals, and those were not good experiences. After Grandmom Strong's funeral, he exploded at Mom that she never liked his mom anyway and was mad for days. When Mom's brother, Carl, who was a deputy sheriff, was killed in action, I made a joking comment to one of my cousins in front of him at the funeral that I was almost big enough to wear his dress shoes. When we got home, he threw them at me and said, "Here. Wear my shoes then since you're so big." What was the big deal about me saying that? I was just kidding around with our relatives. And then when Papa died, he had the ringer on the phone cut off, so the sheriff deputies had to come out to the house to tell Mom her father had died. So she didn't even get to be with him when he passed.

And, that's another fine example he sets. As a repairman for the telephone company, he is supposed to be available during storms. But if he doesn't feel like going out, he makes me answer the phone and lie and say he's not home. So at least that was one thing I've become really good at—telling a lie. It comes pretty natural now without much thought. Then, he put that switch on the phone where he could flip the ringer off, so we wouldn't hear it ring. Nice work example. I'm sure he was probably proud of it. Just like when he brags about parking his work van on the side of the road and taking a nap while he's on the clock.

I don't know how he's kept his job anyway, especially the way he drinks. Comes home, eats, drinks a couple of beers, and then goes to sleep on the couch. Same on most weekends, except then he sleeps on the back porch, watching me work. I don't think I'll ever be able to sit on a couch. Reminds me too much of him laying there sleeping. I'm afraid it would swallow me up like him. At least he leaves us alone though when he's asleep.

***

I wonder if he classifies as an alcoholic, Wes thought as he turned around at the end of the yard and got a glimpse of his father downing the last of his current can of beer.

I guess that depends on your definition of "alcoholic." If it's somebody whose drinking hurts everybody else in the family, then he definitely qualifies. If it's somebody who gets up in the middle of the night and pees into a clothes drawer thinking it's a toilet, then he qualifies on that one too. I don't know.

And on and on it goes in his head, free-falling deeper and deeper into his well of despair, as if he had been thrown out of a plane without a parachute. The constant angry thoughts and bad memories just kept coming like a never-ending waterfall of hurt. *Why do I keep doing this to myself?* Wes thought. *What have I done, God? What am I doing wrong? Show me what I'm supposed to do. I go to church. I make good grades and stay out of trouble. Please answer me. Please. Yeah, that's what I thought. Silence. Always silence from above. Maybe he's right. No wonder I can't play football. Not good for anything.*

Wes didn't welcome or relish these thoughts. He also knew these conversations with himself did absolutely no good, but once the pity party started, there was no stopping it. It was just an endless hailstorm of thoughts to try to make sense of things. And they weren't every day. It was just the overwhelming question of "Why?" when his father had one of his blowouts. Even the noise of the lawnmower couldn't drown out or mow down the ugliness flowing through his head. He continued to go back and forth across the yard in neat rows, trying to make sense of his not-so-neat life. On and on it went. Too many questions. Too few answers.

Glancing at the porch, his father had fallen asleep in his chair with his feet propped up on the rail and an empty beer can at his feet.

CHAPTER 2

GOTTA RUN

The one thing Wes did have was running. Ever since he was knee-high to a grasshopper, he had liked to run. Leave him outside in the sunshine, and he could run all day. Whichever sport was in season, he was game for as long as he could keep moving—baseball, football, or basketball. He loved to organize games in the neighborhood with the other guys. Anything to stay away from home. But getting away was not always that easy.

During the week after school was the best time because his father would not be home from work till five o'clock. But on the weekends, there was always at least one task that had to be completed before he could leave the yard, if at all. Cut the grass. Rake the pine straw. Hold the ladder. Split wood. Pick up pinecones or rocks. Chop a stump. Paint. It was like his father always had something there for him to do to punish him or teach him some lesson or just to keep him busy. His friends would be begging for him to come and play, but Wes would have to tell them to go on before they made it worse. He would try to be there as soon as he could.

It wasn't that he minded helping. It was just that it always felt like he was being punished for something. Told to do it in anger. There was no give and take or negotiating with his father. His way or the highway. And it seemed he was almost always angry. Like the time last summer when Wes was invited to go to the lake on the weekend with his friend Jason and Jason's family. His mom said okay since his dad had gone to the hardware store. Well, Wes was supposed to cut the grass in the backyard that afternoon. They were having so much fun teaching Wes how to ski that Jason's parents lost track of time, and they didn't get Wes home until almost dark. His dad was furious.

"I'll do it first thing Monday," Wes had offered.

"No, you won't," his dad exploded. "You'll get up at eight in the morning and do it."

"But that's Sunday morning. I've got church," Wes pleaded.

"I don't care what day it is. Do it or I'll cut you off," was the reply.

Not cutting grass on Sunday had always been the unspoken eleventh commandment in the Bible Belt South. You just didn't do it. What would the neighbors think? Wes knew his dad could care less about going to church on Sunday, but Wes always went with his mom. He knew he couldn't ask his mom for help or his father might turn on her. He'd just have to get up as early as he could and finish as quickly as he could, so they wouldn't be late.

But that would create another problem. How would Wes shower off after cutting the grass? Better not wake his dad up on Sunday. That was his morning to sleep late. He would usually just be getting up and dressed when they would be returning from church.

And what about washing his hair after cutting the grass? That was another battlefield. His dad believed that your hair should only be washed once a week and that was on Saturday. No matter how sweaty you had gotten or whose nasty football helmet or hat you had worn. Once in junior high, Wes had developed sores in his head during football season from all the sweat and only being able to wash his hair once a week. His mom got a special soap, and that was the only time he had ever been allowed to shampoo more than once a week. If his father suspected that Wes was washing his hair in the shower, he would barge into the bathroom to find out. More than once, Wes had gotten a spanking in the shower when he got caught breaking this commandment. As he got older, he had learned to wash his hair with regular soap at school after sports practice. Or if there was no practice, he would wash his hair in the sink at home before his father got home from work.

So sports and running were his chance to escape to another world for a while. Playing football, basketball, baseball, or just running. It didn't matter. Just as long as he could get away from home and be with his friends outside. Wes ran to and from the games all over their small neighborhood. And if there wasn't a game to be found, he just ran. It was his one time to be free. Free of his father and his moods and his rules. He wasn't even aware that he was exercising or working his body. He just knew it felt good to go.

Running was his only escape. And he often thought of escaping while running—running away and not going back. But where would he go? Maybe to some relatives in Georgia? Wes often wondered what it would be like to live with someone else, but he knew that if he did go through with it, they would turn him in. In the long run, that would make it worse on him and his mom. He definitely didn't want to make it any harder on her, but sometimes it felt good to dream about it as he ran. It was like dreaming, but he wasn't sleeping. He'd let his mind go and get so into the dream that after a little while, he'd look around at where he had run to and didn't remember what he had passed along the way. And he'd just have to smile.

Those were the days of running just for the pure, perfect enjoyment of it. His legs just flowed, not thinking of the effort or the strain. At that point, there really was no strain. Wes felt like he could run forever without tiring. He didn't push himself unless he was in the middle of a game. However, when he was just running to run or travel, he had a steady, untiring pace. It was what every adult runner seeks to recapture—the purity of youthful running with no pressure.

However, as time went on and he got older, his running began to take on another darker aspect. He began to search for understanding about why his father treated him like he did. Why? Would he ever get an answer? With his father constantly putting him down, he began to struggle with self-confidence. It overflowed into other areas. While playing sports in the neighborhood, he had always been one of the older, bigger, and better kids. When he got into school sports at Walhalla Junior High School, he was middle of the pack at best.

It was hard to take the criticism of the other guys there and also not to have the support of his father. Anytime his father got mad about something, he usually threw out hurtful, critical words about his athletic ability. They both stung and stuck like a bumblebee's stinger. His father's words, "No wonder you can't," along with the ribbing of the other guys, began to fester and grow together deep in his soul to where his confidence was slowly rotting away like spoiling fruit. When he ran sometimes, the negative thoughts echoed around in his head like a broken record, and he began to run to hurt. He wanted the pain of running to erase the pain of the negative thoughts. Was it punishment for his perceived athletic shortcomings? Or was he running to prove them wrong? He slowly became a player in the age-old game of "Are we running from something or to something?" He was definitely beginning to try to run away from the pain in his life. It became a deep reservoir of fuel that was feeding a yet to be touched, unquenched fire. He wasn't aware of the reservoir at that time, but it would become the dark secret of future success.

Why do we run? It's the question all runners must eventually face, like a mirror they must eventually peer into. Oh, it always starts out for fun or exercise or to belong to a group. How many runners start out as casual runners in high school because their friends are joining the cross-country team or because they want to meet a certain member of the opposite sex? Maybe they like the view running behind members of the other sex. As they get in better shape over time, they begin to find out they are pretty good at it. Then, they might become the "chased" and not the "chasee" as their stock rises. After all, the best on the team always gets the most desirable members of the other sex. It's just survival of the fittest.

It's the same with older runners who start out running for exercise to maybe get in better shape or lose a little weight. A friend then talks them into running a local 5K. They resist at first, but then they decide to give it a try. What could it hurt? Lo and behold, they place in their age group. The fire is lit. Or maybe someone who has run a little with his kids or played other sports decides if he is ever going to get that marathon under his belt, he better go ahead and give it a try. Or maybe a friend dies, and he decides to run a marathon in the friend's memory as part of a charity like Team in Training. The big day arrives, they survive, and they decide it wasn't so bad after all. Done. Check that off the bucket list.

Then another runner says, "Did you know you missed qualifying for Boston by just a few minutes?"

"Boston?" he replies. "Wow. Me, Boston? No way." Caught: hook, line, and sinker.

From there, it becomes an obsession. Many runners have said, "As long as I'm competitive and keep winning awards, I'll stick with it." It just keeps fueling the fire. Or they have said, "I've worked too hard to get this fit. I don't want to lose it."

And so it was with Wes. It would be many years before he would fully understand what fueled his desire to run. What started out so innocently eventually took on a life of its own. It would eventually reach a good place, but along the way, there would be many ups and downs and stops and starts. He never had a goal of racing or running on a team. "I'm sure everyone else is faster than me anyway," he always told himself when the slightest thought of competing came up. In those easily embarrassed adolescent years, you didn't have to worry about getting embarrassed if you didn't try. *No use adding extra misery to life*, he thought. He had tried playing football to win his father's approval since that seemed to be important to him. He liked it well enough in his younger years, but by the time he got to junior high, and most everyone else was bigger than him, the fun was waning. Sitting on the bench was no fun. And getting banged on in practice was definitely not a joyride. Wes had trudged on in hopes that his turn would come. When he reached the tenth grade, he did get to play some on the JV team, but as fate would have it, his father was away at a technical school for several of the weeks when he was playing.

He wouldn't come when I wasn't playing, and now he can't come. What a waste, Wes thought.

As his tenth-grade year wound down, Wes decided to give up football. He didn't relish the thought of trying to play for Coach Bolton on the varsity. Coach Bolton was a football legend in the state. He had coached almost forty years and won several state titles. "Lightning Bolt" was what the players called him behind his back. And, when he grabbed you by the facemask and started yelling at you and jerking your head around like a bobble head doll, you definitely felt like you had been struck by lightning. Wes felt that because of his size, he would have a rough time on the varsity team, and he had enough hardship at home. No use getting a second helping at school.

While he was trying to decide whether to continue playing football, a friend began talking to him about running cross-country. Jason had been his friend since junior high. Jason had started running cross-country in the ninth grade and was a middle-of-the-pack runner who usually finished in fourth or fifth place. He was a funny, easygoing guy who Wes had always liked. They had never done much together outside of school. Wes was always reluctant to have friends over to his house since he never knew what kind of mood his father would be in. Their contact had been limited mostly to school and a few outings to the lake with Jason's family.

Jason said, "If you're not going to play football, why don't you at least give cross-country a try. I've seen you run in PE, so I know you could do it. You'd fit right in. It's low pressure. Coach Owings is a great guy and easy enough to get along with. He's trying to get more folks on the team, so I'm sure he'd love to have you. Hey, and there are some pretty cute girls on the girls team!"

"You practice together?" Wes asked curiously.

"We warm up together and travel together to meets, but at practice, we don't always do the same runs or workouts. But there is plenty of contact. Bet you didn't have too many girls at football practice, huh?"

"No." Wes laughed. "I'll think about it." Of course, his big concern was what his father's reaction would be to Wes not playing football. When he finally made up his mind and told his father, his reaction was pretty much what he expected.

"Whatever. You weren't playing much anyway. I figured you'd chicken out when you got to Coach Bolton. But don't think you're giving up that job at the drugstore either."

Little did Wes know that he was about to embark on a life-changing adventure. Running was about to take him places he had never dreamed of—good and bad.

CHAPTER 3

CROSS-COUNTRY

J ust as Jason had predicted, Coach Owings was glad to have Wes on the team. "The more, the merrier," he said as he welcomed Wes to the first practice in the fall of eleventh grade. Wes was not the only new face on the team. They had five guys back from the year before and eight new ones.

Jason told Wes not to worry about the new guys because half of them would quit. "They always do after they sweat a little bit." Jason laughed. "Sure hope the cute girls stick around though. Look at 'em. Wow!"

Coach Owings asked Wes if he had ever run or raced before. "No sir, just in football and around the neighborhood."

"Okay, then. We won't kill you. We'll bring you along slowly. I'm sure a lot of these guys aren't in shape, and we have about six weeks before the first meet, so there is some time. The main thing at first is to just enjoy it and work on getting in shape. We'll work on speed later."

After the first practice, Wes asked Jason about the meets. "I know a 5K is 3.1 miles, but who runs and how to you score?"

Jason explained, "Everybody gets to run at all the meets, except the state meet where only the top seven get to run. So that's why there is no pressure. Everybody participates, which is pretty cool. You just decide how hard you want to push yourself and what your goals are. Coach Owings is pretty good about trying to motivate each person to just be the best runner they can be. He knows we can't all run a 5K in under sixteen minutes, which is a very fast time. As far as the scoring, it's pretty simple. The person who finishes first overall gets one point for his team and the second-place person overall gets two points for his team and so on. The points are added up for the top five runners on each team, and the lowest team score wins. If there is a tie, they include the sixth runner. So to have a good team, it's pretty important to have some faster runners in the six, seven, and eight spots. They can bump the other teams' guys down and make their score higher. Make sense?"

Wes nodded as he began to process how it all worked. "Sounds pretty cool."

The next six weeks went by pretty fast as the team did mostly five-to-six-mile runs daily after school to get everybody in shape. The last two weeks before the first meet, they began to do some track workouts where they sprinted varying distances to try to gain some speed along with their endurance. Wes was used to this kind of workout from running sprints at football practice. He usually stayed in the middle of the pack and found the workouts not overly taxing.

Jason was right in that four of the guys quit, but they had never played any sports. That left ten guys on the team. Of the six returning runners, two who were now seniors had been all-region the year before—Adam White and Burt Dunn. "Batman and Robin" they were called because their first names were the same as the actors on the TV show. Looking at the rest of the guys, Wes hoped maybe he could be in the top six. Jason had been the number four runner the year before, but Wes wasn't sure he could beat him. The number three runner had graduated, so

Jason hoped to take his spot. Regardless, Wes thought, *We all get to run in the meets. And this is a whole lot better than getting beat up by the bigger guys at football practice and then not getting to play in the games.*

The first meet always involved all the teams in the region and was known as the region's "Get to Know You Meet." It was held on the course where the end-of-season region championship meet would be held, and it gave everybody a chance to check out the competition. That year, it was at Emerald High School in Greenwood. The only catch, Jason said, was that some teams never run hard at that meet so as to not show what they had. Sandbaggers they were called.

"Doesn't matter to me," Wes replied. "I just want to survive without throwing up or worse."

"You'll be fine," Jason replied. "Just stick with me."

Wes was pretty nervous as he toed the line for his first competitive race. Emerald's course was on the grounds of a children's orphanage. *What a mass of guys*, he thought as he looked around the field at the guys from the other schools. *There must be close to a hundred guys out here.* He shouldered up to Jason as they got ready to start. During the brief pause, he couldn't help noticing several crows at the top of a pine tree on the edge of the course. Their haunting chant sounded just like "can't, can't" being repeated over and over. This reminded him of his father saying, "No wonder you can't play football." For some reason, from that day forward, he would always associate crows with that thought. He looked down and scratched at the ground with his foot as the words rattled around in his head.

Jason elbowed him and said, "Wes, you ready, man?"

"Sorry, zoned out there a minute. Yeah, let's do this."

When the gun went off, it was pretty much what Wes expected with a hundred testosterone-pumped guys being let out of a stable. Some pushing and shoving occurred as everybody tried to run his own pace without getting run over or pushed into the guys in front of him. It took a good half mile before the pack began to thin out enough for Wes to feel like he could run free without bumping elbows with another runner. He noticed he was breathing really hard. He wasn't sure if it was nerves or whether he was running too fast to try to keep up with the guys ahead of him. He had lost track of Jason in the sea of runners as he tried to stay on his feet.

The course had started on a big open field in front of a church on the grounds of the home, and after making a big circle around the field, it soon headed off into the woods. The course began to narrow, and you were locked in by the runners ahead of you. There wasn't much room to pass, even if you wanted to. Wes was not interested in passing at the present time anyway, so it didn't matter to him. He was just in survival mode. His lungs were on fire, and his legs were already hurting. *So this is what it feels like to race*, he thought. He had experienced that feeling before on bad days at home when he would run from his house, his father, his pain. *Interesting*, Wes thought as he compared that feeling to the feeling of competitive racing.

The runners soon popped out of the woods and onto a gravel road that skirted the edge of the property. There were a few parents there, and he heard someone yell, "Halfway there!"

Halfway? I may lose a lung before then! He couldn't see anybody on his team. *I sure hope there aren't this many runners at every meet. This is way too crowded.*

The gravel road soon gave way to a sidewalk that went around the front of the orphanage. The conglomeration of runners began to thin out a little more as some runners picked up the pace and others fell off. Wes wasn't sure which group he fit in or if he was moving up or not. He was just trying to hang on as the burning in his lungs was soon surpassed by the pain in his quads. There was a short, steep hill ahead, and he thought he saw Jason a little ways ahead. Wes tried to push his pace to see if he could catch him. He thought he could have caught his friend if he had a little more time, but the finish line suddenly appeared. His first race was over.

The finish area looked like a war zone. Wes slowly walked around and surveyed the carnage as he tried to catch his breath. Bodies were everywhere. Some were on their backs about to pass out, gasping for precious oxygen. The ones who were standing looked as if they were about to throw up. Some did unceremoniously. Nobody cared how they looked. It was over, and they had survived. There was no doubt most of the fellows had given their all. As the finishers continued to come in, the level of effort seemed to drop off. Wes wondered if these were the guys that were sandbagging or the guys who weren't that serious about their running or just weren't in shape yet.

Jason suddenly slapped Wes on the back and said, "Well, you did it. You are now officially a runner." He poured a cup of water over Wes's head. "What did you think?"

Wes shook his head and replied, "Too many people. I hope it's not always like that. Other than that, it was great."

Coach Owings ran up and high-fived both of them. "Good job, guys. You were three and four for the team. Both just under seventeen minutes. Not sure how we did overall, but this one doesn't really matter. It will depend on the guys behind you." Looking at Jason, but pointing to Wes, Coach said, "I'm not sure where you found this guy, but I think we got a keeper." They all laughed together before Coach ran off to find his other runners.

At the next meet a week later, there were only three local teams. It was much different for Wes. It was not nearly as crowded, and he could see all the other runners ahead of him. He liked this feeling of being able to run free and not being boxed in by other runners around him. He stayed right behind Jason the whole way and felt much better as they finished third and fourth for the team again and overall. Batman and Robin were first and second, of course, and their team swept the top four places. Everyone was excited about winning their first meet of the season.

In the next several meets, Wes finished just behind Jason. The meet the following week would include the top three teams from the region and would go a long way toward deciding who would be in the driver's seat for the region title. Wes was beginning to get used to the routine of distance and speed workouts, and his body was adjusting nicely. *This sure is a lot more fun than football.* He liked Coach Owings and the other guys, and he was glad he had made the switch no matter what his father might have to say.

The meet went as the others had; Wes finished behind Jason. Batman and Robin were ahead of them, but not by much. The team finished a close second. Wes felt good, and he felt like he was getting stronger without being overly spent.

Afterward, Coach Owings came up and grabbed Wes by the arm. "Let's talk."

They walked away from the other guys, and Coach said, "What are you doing?"

Wes frowned and said, "What do you mean?"

"Well, I see a guy who is on cruise control. You look pretty fresh when you get through. Making it look pretty easy. Is this the way you want it? To just cruise through each meet, finishing behind Jason every time?"

"No, no," Wes stammered. "I'm doing the best I can, Coach."

"I don't think so, Wes. I think you probably can do better if you push yourself. Why are you holding back?"

"I'm not." Wes looked down and pawed at the ground with his right foot.

Coach kept pushing. "Talk to me, Wes."

"Coach, um, I'm the new guy. Batman and Robin are seniors. It's their year to shine, and I definitely don't want to offend Jason. He's my friend."

Coach frowned. "Wes, what do you think these guys will think when they find out we could have won today if you had given it your all? Sure, they want to be the top dogs on the team, but they want to earn it. They don't want someone to give it to them. And they definitely want to win the region no matter where they finish for the team. You look like you have a gift. Use it. A famous runner, Steve Prefontaine, said "To not do your best is to sacrifice the gift." He's right. No holding back, okay?"

"Okay," Wes replied sheepishly.

CHAPTER 4

RINGER

The next practices followed the same script. Wes continued to work hard, but he didn't show any signs of being a potential threat to the school record time in cross-country. He could feel Coach watching him closely, and it made him uncomfortable. It made Wes feel like he had committed a crime, and Coach knew and was waiting for him to confess.

The upcoming meet would feature the top runner in the upstate, Abdi Montohan, who was from Daniel High School. He was an Ethiopian orphan who had been adopted by some Christian missionaries who ran the Baptist Student Union at Clemson University. Abdi was fast, very fast. He was becoming somewhat of a legend in the upstate for his running ability. To make matters worse, the meet was on Daniel's home course.

The night before the meet, Wes did not sleep well. His father had one of his episodes after Wes had gone to bed. He heard his father in his parents' bedroom, cussing his mother out at the top of his lungs. Wes crossed his hands and prayed over and over for it to stop. He squeezed his hands together so tight that he could feel his fingers going numb. After listening to the outburst for at least twenty minutes, Wes heard a thump. He heard his mom cuss his father in return, which was unusual. He got up, went to their door, and peeked in. His mother was on her knees and leaning against the bed. She quickly told Wes to go back to bed as his father gave him an angry glare. Things settled down after that, but Wes stayed awake and wondered if his father had hit her. What, if anything, could he do to protect his mother and improve the situation? Wes felt like he needed to do something, but what should he do? He eventually drifted off to sleep as the thoughts raced around in his head.

Before the meet, Coach Owings gathered his guys for a pep talk. He talked about not being intimidated by Abdi and especially about not going out too fast. "Don't let the adrenaline get to you, and don't try to keep up with this guy from the start. He likes to go out fast, hoping you will try to keep up, and then when you fade in the last third of the race, his teammates will pick you off. That's how they get such low scores." Then, he said something that Wes felt was directed toward him as much as anybody else on the team. "Guys, there is a wall of pain you all have to bust through to be the best you can be. Toward the end of the race when you feel like you can't go anymore and you just want it to be over, if you reach deep and find another gear, you might just be amazed at what is possible. The sky is the limit. I challenge you to bust through that wall and see what you are capable of achieving."

When they got to the start line, Wes took his usual place beside Jason. He looked to his left and carefully studied Abdi. The guy looked like a Kenyan sprinter straight out of a running magazine. He was tall and very thin, but the thing that impressed Wes the most was how long and thin his legs were. *Boy, I bet he can cover some ground quickly with those wheels*, he thought. His gaze soon went beyond Abdi to Coach standing just beyond the start line. He was staring Wes down. When their eyes met, Coach began to nod slowly as if to say, "You can do it. Let's see it.'

When the gun went off, it was just as Coach had said with Abdi going out like a gazelle. Batman and Robin both took off as if they had not heard a word of Coach's instructions. There is something about being a teenage guy hyped up on testosterone and wanting to prove yourself that will make you throw all caution to the wind. After all, it was the dynamic duo's last season, and they had something to prove. Wes stayed with Jason in the middle of the pack as usual. He felt good, and thank goodness Jason had listened to Coach. Wes didn't know what he would have done if Jason had gone out with their crazy teammates.

It was the typical course that started beside the practice fields behind Daniel High School and went into the woods for a little ways before it came back out on the sidewalk in front of the school. Most high school campuses were just about the right size for a 5K race. They covered about ten to twenty acres and usually had a patch of woods on the border that could be incorporated into a cross-country course. After all, what is a cross-country course without some *country*?

After they went into the woods, the pack bunched up. Wes lost sight of Abdi and the others. He felt pretty much like he had at the other races—not too fast and not too slow. Wes was looking forward to reaching some open stretch to see if he could pass some of the pack. When they finally came out of the woods at about the halfway point and headed around toward the front of the school on the sidewalk, Coach was waiting. He began to run a few yards with Wes and the pack as if he had something to say. He was only a few feet to Wes's right when he finally said, "Show me something, Wes. You can do this."

At the same time, Wes heard a flock of crows dismally cawing nearby and the voice of his father saying, "No wonder you can't play football." It just kept ringing in his head, "No wonder you can't. No wonder you can't." Wes thought of the events of the night before, and he suddenly felt that old familiar anger welling up inside of him that had fueled him on some of his suicide sprints at home when he just wanted to get away. It was the frustration of being in a situation at home that he had no control over and could not change. Oblivious to his surroundings and the other runners, Wes suddenly took off like he never had before. He just went as hard as he could like he had been shot out of a cannon. Anger poured from his brain into his legs. It was as if by transferring the pain from his brain to his legs, he could overcome those negative, hurtful thoughts and wash it all away. All he felt was anger exploding through his body.

"I'll show you," Wes repeated silently over and over to fight back his father's voice. Before he knew it, he had left Jason and the pack. He quickly covered a lot of ground. As he made the left turn ahead to go back to the fields behind the school, he was amazed to see Batman and Robin ten yards ahead. And about forty yards ahead of them was Abdi. The anger and frustration continued to surge through his body as he thought, *I'll show everybody—Dad, Coach, everybody.*

Wes began to feel the burning in his lungs, but this was one time he did not care. *I do not care if I drop dead out here. Nobody would care anyway.* They headed toward the finish line on the soccer fields just ahead. Ironically, the more his body hurt physically, the better he felt in his head psychologically; it was as if the pent-up pain was leaving him. It was as if he was temporarily erasing or numbing it. He was closing hard on Batman and Robin. He heard their labored breathing as he went by them, and he knew they were done. Only Abdi remained.

Wes quickly realized the finish line was just ahead—and he was running out of time. Surging as hard as he could, he closed to within ten feet of Abdi as he crossed the finish line. Collapsing on the ground just beyond the finish line, Wes was a totally spent, heaving puddle of emotion. He would have broken into tears if he could have caught his breath. All he could do was gasp for air.

What just happened? He slowly realized he had just finished second overall. *How did I do that?*

Before his oxygen-starved mind could process an answer, Batman and Robin were on him like white on rice. "Rookie, don't you ever do that again," Batman screamed as they stood over him.

"I'm sorry. I'm sorry," Wes said between gasps for air.

"Sorry? You're sorry all right," Batman replied. "Don't you ever hold back on us again. You could have had him, you sandbagger."

"What?" Wes mumbled. He thought he must be hallucinating. Not enough oxygen. "You're not mad?"

"Yes, we're mad," Batman and Robin said together.

"We could be scoring so much better as a team if you hadn't been holding out on us. We could win the region if you'll run like that. Don't ever hold back again! Do you understand?" Batman said between laughs.

"Okay, okay." Wes laughed on the ground, gasping for air.

Suddenly, two other bodies came crashing on the scene. Coach and Jason arrived simultaneously and fell to their knees on either side of Wes.

"That was amazing," Jason screamed. "Just amazing."

"I knew it. I knew it," Coach yelled. "We've got a ringer! Wes, you just ran a 15:44. That's over a minute faster than you had been running."

Wes smiled. *Maybe I can do something.*

CHAPTER 5

CHAMP (ALMOST)

The rest of that season followed a new script following Wes's newfound motivation. Wes became the guy to beat, and he finished first for the team and first at almost every meet the rest of the season. The team won the region, and Wes captured the championship as the overall fastest runner. At the state championship, he finished fourth overall. Abdi ran away with the title. Batman and Robin finished eighth and ninth overall, which allowed the team to be tenth in the state, which was their highest finish ever. The team and Coach Owings were thrilled with the team's performance. Based on the good crop of returners for the next season, expectations would be high for an even better finish.

The summer before his senior season was an up and down one for Wes. He continued in his part-time job at the drugstore to keep his dad off of his back and to pay for gas and other car expenses. It also gave him a legitimate excuse to stay away from home. He did what he was told as far as work around the house, but he also knew that if his dad saw him idle at home he would find something for him to do. So, he took odd jobs cutting the neighbor's grass.

Wes ran in the mornings to fulfill the training regimen Coach Owings had given each of the guys, sometimes with Jason but mostly alone. He enjoyed the freedom and solitude running alone gave him. He could run as far and as fast as he wanted, and he could use the time to think or vent his frustrations with his father. It wasn't all bad; his father did take him fishing occasionally. These were the times his father seemed more at peace and less angry at the world, but there continued to be episodes that showed his true colors.

Like the time they went to fish about forty miles away at the Clark's Hill Dam. His father wanted to go there to see if they could catch any bigger fish that might be coming through the spillway below the dam. He had heard stories of twenty-pound bass being caught there. When they arrived, two older black men were packing up to leave.

Wes and his father got out of their car. Wes's father waved and said, "Hey, John. John, y'all catch anything? Do any good, John?"

"No, sir. No, sir. Not today," they replied.

"Okay, John," his father replied.

Wes was impressed that his father knew their names and was talking to them in a friendly manner since he seldom spoke to African-Americans.

Wes asked, "How do you know those men?"

"I don't know them." His father laughed. "They all answer to John."

Suddenly, Wes wanted to hide and not be seen with his father. *How embarrassing and degrading that must have been to those men,* he thought. He felt so bad for them. *But I should have known as racist as he is.*

At least his father seemed to be treating his mother a little better. They went out to eat together occasionally, and there didn't seem to be as many explosions of anger. Wes began to feel like maybe he was the reason for his father's anger. The less he was around his father, the better it seemed to be. He never could figure out what his father had against him. Why the anger? He knew his grandfather abandoned his father's family when his father was five years old, so he wondered if it was anger at not having a father of his own. Or maybe it was just the fact that he never had a fatherly example of his own, and he just didn't know how to be a loving father. Or was it just rage at the pressures of life? Wes would never know for sure.

And then there was the trip they took to Georgia to visit some relatives that summer. His father had been drinking beer all weekend while fishing and did not want to drive home, so he let Wes drive. To keep from having to stop periodically to empty his swollen bladder, his father decided he would urinate in a cup as they drove and just pour it out the window. Wes could not believe he was thinking of doing this and told him they had plenty of time to stop. Undaunted, his father went ahead with his plan, and as he poured it out the window, it blew back in as a spray on his mother in the backseat. She was understandably mad, which made for a nice three-hour ride home. Wes swore right then that he would never travel with them again, and he didn't.

All in all, though, the summer went pretty well for Wes. He was busy, but he figured that wasn't a bad thing. He never dated because he still felt behind in the game since he had started driving later than everyone else. And he was pretty shy around girls anyway. He was looking forward to school, not because of his classes, but because he was anxious to see how the cross-country season would go. His success in the previous season had given him some much-needed confidence, and it was nice to be known as good at something. Positive attention always lifts the spirits.

The season went by like a flash. Wes was still the man to beat in the region after winning the championship the previous year. He was not going to sneak up on anyone this year though. Jason was now a strong number-two runner since he had worked hard over the summer also. They had a couple of younger new guys who were pretty fast, and they were hoping to finish at least top five in the state. Coach Owings was very optimistic and excited. He had been very supportive to Wes and was a positive male role model that Wes sorely needed.

Coach had even told Wes that he needed to decide about running in college; if Wes was interested, they would begin to contact some college coaches. This encouragement was very motivational to Wes since no one in his family had ever graduated from college, and he had always hoped for a white-collar career. He had assumed the best he could hope for was living at home and maybe commuting to Clemson, which was thirty minutes away. With his father's periodic threats to cut him off ringing in his head, Wes was determined to pay his own tuition or get a loan, so he would not be dependent on him. That thought made the chance at a scholarship somewhere sound very appealing.

Wes did not disappoint his senior season. He swept the region meets and the region championship easily. Jason had a great season also and finished second in every meet but two. The newcomers held their own, allowing the team to win the region for the second year in a row. Wes, of course, won the region championship again and was Runner of the Year in the region, and he and Jason won all-region honors. Coach Owings said Wes's run at the region meet was one of the best races he had ever seen as three runners from Seneca worked together to box Wes in early to allow their best runner to take a commanding lead. Wes was finally able to break free from their trap as they began to tire midway, and he quickly closed the gap on the leader. It looked like it would be a tight finish, but with two hundred yards left, Wes turned on the jets and won easily. This progress and success was all a confidence booster for Wes, but he still had unfinished business at the state championship.

Coach Owings was prepping him for the state championship by saying that Abdi again would be his main competition. They had not had to race against each other this season because Daniel High School had been moved to another region, so it would be an interesting duel. And memorable it was. It would also be the first time Wes's father had seen him run.

It was a beautiful day during the first weekend in November. The course, as always, was on the sand hills of Columbia at the Clemson Research Park. It was a sandy, woodland course with a challenging hill less than half a mile from the finish.

Wes felt good and ran strong. He was determined to stay within striking distance of Abdi, and he did just that. He never let him get more than a few short yards ahead of him, and the rest of the field was in hot pursuit. Just past the 2.5-mile mark was "The Hill," a thirty-foot steep killer of dreams that separated the men from the boys. Wes found himself in a pack of six lead runners that included Abdi. Wes, Abdi, and a runner from Wando crested the hill ahead of the others, leaving just over two hundred yards of dry, sandy field to decide the winner. The cheers of the crowd were deafening at that point as parents, coaches, and fans all tried to encourage their runner to the tape first. Wes was just a couple of steps behind Abdi as they began to pull away from the third runner. They both were sprinting at top speed and trying to summon every ounce of energy they had to break the tape first.

Then, thirty yards from the finish, something happened that was straight out of a fairy tale. The toes of Abdi's left foot caught a clump of grass, and he lost his balance. The strain of the race and especially the last hill had robbed him of his coordination, and he began to flail his arms wildly in a desperate effort to keep his feet.

So close, Abdi must have been thinking. *Just have to make it a little further. Keep your feet.*

Just behind him to his right, Wes watched in stunned amazement at what was happening. Could this be his chance to sprint ahead and gain glory—the state championship? These things happen so suddenly that there is no time to debate how to react, but it is said that someone's true character will appear in these split-second instances. To the utter shock and amazement of everyone watching, as Wes caught up to Abdi, he reached down with his left hand to his stumbling opponent, grabbed him by the upper right arm, and pulled him up to help him regain his balance. It all happened in a split second on the dead run. Abdi quickly straightened back up into top speed and crossed the tape just one step ahead of Wes.

Wes and Abdi collapsed on their backs, totally spent after their championship effort. Both runners were motionless for several minutes, gasping for air as a crowd gathered around them, clapping boisterously.

Abdi eventually stood up to a cheer, and he helped Wes to his feet to an even louder cheer. He hugged Wes tightly and said in English thick with a North African accent, "Thank you, my friend. You are a true champion." He grabbed Wes's hand in his and lifted it into the air. The applause was thunderous and went on for several minutes as the two champions smiled.

Coach Owings finally broke through the crowd and gave Wes a big bear hug. With tears running down his cheeks, he said, "That was the most courageous thing I have ever witnessed. I am so proud of you."

Partially still in shock, Wes replied, "I don't know, Coach. I could have won I guess."

Coach Owings took Wes's sweaty face in his hands and looked him straight in the eye. "Listen to me. You did the right thing. Just listen to this crowd. They're cheering for you. Wes, I saw grown men crying at what you did. You are the real champion."

As the crowd eventually turned its attention back to the other runners who were finishing, Wes saw his parents. His mother hugged him and told him she was proud of him.

Wes's father said, "That was pretty stupid. You could have won."

Wes would replay what he did in his mind many times in the future. He would wonder what it would have been like to cross the tape first, but he never doubted that he did the right thing. He would make some bad decisions in the future, but he always knew that in that one shining moment, he had made the right choice. He was always proud of that, and it meant a lot that he had made someone else proud of him besides his mom.

As they were preparing to load the bus after the awards ceremony, Coach Owings walked up to the bus with a thin, athletic man in a Clemson running jacket. "Wes, this is Coach Fields from Clemson. He's the head coach of their cross-country team, and he wants to talk to you just a second."

As he shook Wes's hand, Coach Fields said, "Hi, Wes. You ran a great race, and that was a very courageous thing you did out there at the finish. I was very impressed. You've had a great season, and you're the kind of guy I want on my team if you are interested."

Wes's eyes got big, and his mouth dropped open in stunned silence. Pointing to his chest, he said, "Me?"

"You bet," Coach Fields said with a laugh.

"Yes, yes, absolutely," Wes replied excitedly with a smile that would not come off for several days.

"Great," Coach Fields replied. "Here's my card. Call me next week, and we'll get together to work out the details, okay?"

"Yes, sir. I will. Thank you," Wes replied.

Even his father said later, "Well, maybe second wasn't so bad if you get some college money out of it."

CHAPTER 6

TRAGEDY

The rest of that school year and the following summer crept by. Wes counted the days until he could leave home. Most kids are eager to leave home to gain more freedom, but in Wes's case, it was more to escape the pressure of walking on eggshells. It was always a calculated battle to read his father's expressions and comments and head off explosions. Wes would forever feel like he was pretty good at judging someone's mood by reading tone and facial expressions because of what he had experienced in his childhood.

Wes did get a full athletic scholarship to Clemson, which would allow him to live on campus. He was so thankful because it meant he would not have to live at home and commute. The only thing about that type of scholarship is that it is reevaluated each year and can be lost if you do not perform as expected. For this reason, he dedicated himself over the summer to the training program Coach Fields gave him. He had found his ticket away from his father, and he was determined to make it a one-way ticket.

However, he still could not help worrying about his mother and how she would be without him there. Wes continued to see indications that things might be improving as his parents went out to eat together occasionally and had other positive moments. Wes began thinking it really was him that made his father so angry. *So be it,* he thought. *If it helps, I'll be glad to be out of here.*

Arriving on the Clemson University campus at the end of the summer was a bit of a culture shock for Wes. Nonstop parties, booze, and crazy girls everywhere. Wes had not experienced much of that in high school since he never got out much, and being naturally shy, he tried to avoid as much of it as he could. Even though he liked running, he knew his main reason for being there was to keep his scholarship so he would never have to return home to live. He was determined to focus on his schoolwork and keeping his spot on the team. Thank goodness that his roommate was a shy, reserved computer nerd who was in the Honors College. Wes would not have to worry about Tom putting pressure on him to party. Tom's idea of fun was playing computer games with other geeks in his classes.

The guys on the cross-country team were a curious mix of underachievers and overachievers. Some were partiers who were gifted runners but not too serious about their training and just wanted to wear the uniform. Some were not as gifted but serious about their running and trying to improve. And then some seemed to be from another planet with unbelievable talent and a good work effort. Wes fell into the middle group. He was a late bloomer who had not yet reached his full potential. He was determined to do everything Coach said to be the best he could be. Not having to return home was also a powerful motivator.

Clemson had been in the middle of the pack in the Atlantic Coast Conference the previous season and was hoping to improve this year. Their number one runner, Paul Karabi, was a senior from Kenya, and no one on the team could touch him—he was so fast. Coach had added another freshman, Bo Kusterdam, from

South Africa who had established himself as heir apparent to Paul. Those two fell in the category of being from another planet.

Before the season started, Wes felt he might be able to be the number five or six runner, and the season proved this to be true. His competition, Austin, was one of the gifted but not too serious runners. It drove Wes crazy that this guy could party all the time and still turn out decent times. On top of that, Austin was cocky as all get out. He loved to needle Wes about coming out to party with the other guys. "It'll make you faster," he teased.

At the ACC championship in Raleigh, Clemson finished third. Wes just edged Austin out as the fifth finisher for the team. Everyone was excited about their best showing in years, and with everyone but Paul returning, they had high hopes for future success. Wes was happy to beat out Austin, and by finishing in the top six all season, he would be assured of keeping his scholarship. He felt really good with the way things had gone on the team and was already looking forward to the next season. Wes was dedicated to doing whatever Coach Fields told him to do in the off-season to improve.

Wes's classes were also going well. He had to study hard, and with running, he did not have much extra time. He had decided to major in psychology and thought he might like to teach one day and maybe coach cross-country. Wes had always been curious about how the brain worked and why people thought and acted the way they did. He thought he might be able to figure his father out and keep himself from making the same mistakes. Interesting how people from Wes's background seem to have an interest in understanding what makes people tick. Maybe he just wanted an answer to why his father was like he was. Or maybe he didn't want to end up like him.

Wes Strong had reached the apex of his life up to that point. He had survived his childhood and established himself as a

Division I runner, and his future looked bright. He was happier than he had ever been and just wanted these days to never end. Unfortunately, it would not last.

Just before Wes had left for college, his father has asked him to help pick out a VCR for their home. Wes thought it might be a good idea for his parents to spend time watching movies together. He had no idea what kind of movies his father had in mind until he got a call from his father late on a Friday night in January. His father said his mother had freaked out and was trying to hurt him. He told Wes he better come get her right away. In the background, he heard his mother saying, "It's not true, Wes. It's not me. It's him." His father abruptly hung up the phone.

Wes was stunned. He thought he had seen all of his father's bad episodes in the past, but this was going to a new level. He had never told Wes to remove her. Was he about to hurt her? Or had he already and was afraid he might lose total control? Wes knew he better get there as quickly as possible. He made it in record time—less than twenty minutes for the thirty-mile ride.

When he entered his parents' house, he calmly asked, "What's going on?"

His mother was crying. Through her tears, she said, "I'm not doing those things in those movies. I'm not."

His father suddenly appeared and was belligerent, cussing at the top of his lungs.

Wes was suddenly worried for their safety and tried to calm his father down.

"Get her out now. Now! And I'll shoot the next person through that door—neighbors or relatives. You hear me!"

Trying to calm things, Wes said, "Okay, okay, just let her get some clothes, and we'll leave." Motioning to his mother, he said, "Just grab some things and let's go."

"Wes, no," she said through her tears.

"Now!" his father screamed.

With that his mother turned and hurried to the bedroom. His father sat down in the den and continued to curse under his breath. For the first time, Wes looked around and surveyed the latest damage. He saw several broken vases and dishes and a hole in the wall from something thrown. His concern continued to grow, and he knew they better get out of there quickly before things got worse.

Wes hurried his mother to his car as quickly as he could. "Just take me to Kathy's. I can stay there tonight, I guess," she said as she continued to cry. His mom's best friend was a widow and lived several miles away.

"Okay," Wes said after a minute. Slowly driving away, he asked, "Are you all right?"

"I guess," she said weakly.

"Did he hurt you?"

"I'm okay. He pushed me and tried to choke me," she replied.

"What set him off this time?" Wes asked.

"Those dirty movies," she said. "It's been horrible. That's all he watches on that VCR."

Wes decided he didn't want any more details. There was an awkward silence as they tried to comprehend what had just happened.

What will this mean going forward?

Wes knew he could not be there to protect her all the time if she went back and wondered what he could do. *Is she strong enough to live on her own?* Sleep would be in short supply that night.

Wes knew his father had to work that weekend. The next day, he took his mom back by their house to gather up some clothes and personal things and her car. Entering as usual through the side door, Wes thought it was weird that his father had nailed a short two-by-four to the inside of the side door into the door frame as if to keep them out. He pushed the door open with a little effort, but he worried there might be other booby traps. Who knew what his father was capable of doing?

Wes wanted her to hurry in case his father showed up, but his mother's frayed emotions slowed her to a snail's pace. Wes kept trying to reassure her that it would be all right. For some reason, he couldn't bring himself to hug her. He felt emotionally paralyzed. Maybe it was fear of his father. He just wanted to get her out of there as soon as he could.

After they left, Wes told her she did not have to live that way any longer if she did not want to. "I think you make enough money to support yourself. It's getting worse—and who knows what he might do next time? You will have to decide for yourself though. It's up to you."

His mother slowly replied, "I don't know. I married for life."

"But not if your life is in danger," Wes said. "Just think about it. Kathy said you can stay with her as long as you like. We can work it out."

The following Monday afternoon, Wes got a call from his father. "I've talked to Will, my lawyer, and he said to let it go. So tell your Mom she can come back."

Wes was shocked, but he felt free to speak since he and his mother were out of there. "Me tell Mom? No *I'm sorry* or anything? I think you got it backwards, don't you?"

"Just tell her."

Wes continued, "Look, what I'm telling her is she doesn't have to go back to that kind of life if she doesn't want to. She's taken it long enough. It's up to her."

"Just like that, you're throwing it all away?" his father said.

"I'm not doing anything. It's her decision. I'll support her if she leaves, and hopefully you and I can work things out between us after that," Wes said. "But I can't let your temper hurt her anymore."

"After all I've done for you? You're going to turn on me?" his father asked.

Wes had heard enough and exploded. "All you've done for me? What? What have you done for me? All the yelling and cussing and anger. Spanked the tar out of me as a kid. Told me I was not good at anything, and then when I did try to lift weights for football, you made me walk home. Hardly ever a kind word. Always putting us both down. I wish I had a dime for every time I heard you curse her. Breaking things and cussing. Thanks. Thanks a lot for all you've done for me." Wes broke down in tears.

"Okay. I'll leave y'all alone then," his father said weakly as he hung up.

In the following weeks, his mom continued to work and stay with Kathy. She asked to see a lawyer to get some information, and Wes went with her. They determined that if she did seek a divorce, she would have enough to buy a small condo. She might have to get a part-time job too, but she should be able to make ends meet. In the meantime, his father would call Wes periodically, blaming Wes for what happened and never admitting any guilt of his own. Wes defended himself and told his father he needed to look in the mirror. It was a very stressful time for everyone, but deep down, Wes knew it was long overdue.

Then, the unimaginable happened. His mom had been an emotional wreck at first, but she was slowly coming around and beginning to see that it was for the best. Wes was finally thinking she might be all right on her own as she began making plans for a new future.

Exactly six weeks after Wes's mom had left, he got a phone call from Kathy. "Wes, come quick. Your mom was leaving the neighborhood, and she pulled out in front of a truck. It's bad, Wes. Please hurry."

Wes didn't even hang up. When he got to the emergency room in Walhalla, Kathy met him at the door in tears. "Wes, I'm so sorry. She didn't make it," she said sobbing as she hugged him. "I'm sorry."

"What? How?" Wes would later learn that she stopped at the stop sign, but she evidently didn't see the truck as she pulled out and was struck on the driver's side. The other driver was hurt but would live.

Wes's world came crashing down. He had no one. The only person who loved him unconditionally was gone. All of his grandparents were dead. His father hated him and would probably blame him for this too. As it would end up, his father didn't even go to the funeral. The neighbors said his response was that if she hadn't left him, she would still be alive.

If she hadn't left him? Wes shook his head. *How about if he hadn't kicked her out, she would still be alive. Or if she hadn't left him, he probably would have killed her. It's never his fault. Unbelievable.*

Wes was beside himself with anger. What could he do though? He couldn't change anything. He would never understand his father. It didn't matter now, however. His father might as well be dead too.

CHAPTER 7

BAD DECISIONS

Wes returned to classes after a week. His teammates were very supportive and tried to keep him active to take his mind off things. They ran every day, and Tom made sure he got up and made it to all his classes. No one had to remind Wes that it was more important than ever to keep his grades up and keep his place on the team. That became his all-encompassing focus. Run and study. Run and study. That was his mantra. As if he needed more negative emotions to fuel his running.

Even Austin seemed to be compassionate and sympathetic to what had happened. He made sure Wes was included in the team activities.

About a month after the funeral, four of the guys, including Wes and Austin, went for a run late on a Friday afternoon. They finished up their run in downtown Clemson, stopped at Little Caesar's Pizza, and got a couple of five-dollar pizzas.

Afterward, Austin said there was an outdoor party at the Delta house. "It's on the way back. Let's just stop and grab a beer. We don't have to stay long," he said. The others were in agreement. Wes didn't really want to go, but he didn't want to be alone either.

Wes had never been a drinker because of how he had seen it affect his father. But it was the off-season, and he figured it might help get his mind off his mom. He accepted a cold one when Austin offered it. All the guys sat under the huge oaks behind the Delta house. White Christmas lights dangled from the branches. It didn't feel too bad to Wes as they cut up with some of their other friends. It was a nice break from reality if just for a little while.

After a couple of hours and several beers, they headed back to the dorm in good spirits. Not used to the effects of alcohol, Wes was a little lightheaded. He was not bad—and definitely not drunk. But as they headed across the dark perimeter of the yard, Wes was not as alert as he might have been and did not see the stump hole ahead. He stepped into it with his left foot and heard his ankle pop. He screamed in pain as he hit the ground. The other guys grabbed him and helped him up, giggling and asking if he was okay. They thought he had just tripped. Wes knew it was bad since he could put very little weight on his left foot, but he did not think it was broken. For a minute, they discussed what they should do.

Since Wes did not want to go to the infirmary smelling of beer, they helped him back to his dorm room. That night, he soaked his foot in ice and took some Advil. He sat on the edge of his bed angry at himself for going to the party and wondering what else could go wrong. Staring at his rapidly swelling foot, Wes shook his head. The alcohol in his system soon made him sleepy. After a few minutes, he was fast asleep.

When Wes woke up the next day, his foot was throbbing and swollen. He tried to walk on it and fell back on his bed in pain. Tom took him to the infirmary, and the initial diagnosis was a bad sprain. They called Coach Fields, and he came by. After some discussion, they decided to do an MRI to make sure there was nothing more serious. It showed no broken bones, but there was a torn ligament. Recovery could be long. Wes was in tears when he got the news from the team doctor.

What have I done wrong? Why?

They put in a walking cast and gave him crutches and a strong painkiller containing hydrocodone. Coach took him back to the dorm.

"Get some rest, and be sure to do what the trainers tell you. You'll be fine. It's the off-season, so there is plenty of time."

Wes nodded, but in his mind, he worried about long-term effects on his running and the possibility of losing his spot on the team. He was still angry about going to the party. *If I had just come back. I can't lose my scholarship. Not now. How stupid.*

Wes was determined to get back to running as quickly as possible, so he did everything the trainers told him to do. He went by the trainer's office every day and soaked his ankle in an ice bath. They did some massage of his leg to help get the swelling down. He rode a one-footed stationary bike to lightly exercise his good leg. And he took his painkillers regularly because he had been told they would help with the pain and swelling. They also helped him sleep and kept his mind off his problems. Wes needed all the help he could get in that department. He thought constantly about his mother's death and whether he would be able to run again. His promising future suddenly did not look so secure.

One week slowly turned into two and then three. Wes was able to walk without the crutches. By the fourth week, the swelling was down, and he was allowed to take his walking cast off for several hours per day. His ankle was still very sore and discolored, so he continued to take the painkillers, which the trainers were very willing to supply. He never thought too much about it because he trusted them fully, and they said he needed to keep taking them. Besides, they made him feel better overall and kept his mood elevated. By the sixth week, Wes was allowed to run in place in the swimming pool. He welcomed the positive progress. The trainers told him to start cutting back on the painkillers to begin weaning him off of them, but running in the pool made his ankle hurt. He resisted cutting back.

One of the trainers seemed more sympathetic to this. Bill continued to give prescriptions to Wes for the hydrocodone. Things seemed to be okay as long as he could run in the pool and get his painkillers. Then, one day when he showed up in the training office, Wes was told that Bill had been fired for forging prescriptions for hydrocodone. Wes was shocked. They gave him some over-the-counter ibuprofen. It never occurred to him that Bill might be doing something wrong or that he might have trouble getting off the painkillers. Wes was just doing what he was told to help his ankle heal. When he had trouble sleeping that night, he knew he had to have more than ibuprofen.

The next day, Friday, Wes went back to the trainers early and begged them to get him a few more hydrocodone to help him get through this. They told him that everyone was being watched closely after what had happened to Bill, and there was nothing they could do. They gave him some advice that absolutely did not help: "The weekend is coming up. Get some beer and sleep it off. It will be out of your system by Monday."

"That's what got me in this mess to begin with," Wes told them angrily, but they would not change their mind. "I am not going to survive like this."

Wes tried to go to class, but he was too jittery to pay attention. He left after his first class and went back to his room and tried to sleep. He was sweating profusely, and all he could think about was getting more painkillers. He knew beer would not help. He felt too nauseated to drink anyway.

When Tom returned from his afternoon classes, Wes was throwing up in the toilet. Wes told him what had happened and said he had to find some painkillers.

"Looks like withdrawal man—old fashioned DTs," Tom said.

"I don't care what it is. I've got to have something," Wes said. "Can you help me? Do you know where I can get some pills?"

"I don't know, Wes. You sure you want to do that?"

"It's either that or the hospital, and I can't let coach see me like this," Wes replied between gasps. "I just need a few to help wean me off."

"Okay, let me call some friends." Tom may have been a nerd, but even nerds in college have friends who like to party.

After a few phone calls, Tom said, "I might have found somebody who will sell you some. He's a friend of a friend. I don't know him personally. He hangs out in the back room of The Library. His name is Willie T. Tell him you know Walt." The Library was a bar downtown so named that when parents asked what their kids had been doing, they could honestly say they had been at "the library."

"Thanks," Wes said. "I'll go now."

Wes had only been in The Library a couple of times, but he knew the back room that Tom was talking about. Wes cleaned up and hobbled downtown. It was early on Friday afternoon, and he was betting that Willie would be there already. Stumbling into the darkened bar, Wes headed to the back. He found a group of guys drinking beer at a table. He asked one of them if Willie was there. He nodded to a long-haired, dreadlocked white guy who looked like he might be a grad student.

As Wes stepped toward Willie, a black guy wearing shades grabbed Wes by the arm and said, "Who wants to know?"

"My name's Wes. I was hoping I could get some pain pills."

"What makes you think we got pills, man?" The guy didn't let go of Wes's arm.

"Walt sent me," Wes quickly said.

Willie nodded. "What you need, my man?" Willie asked.

"Hydrocodone," Wes said. "I hurt my foot, and now the trainers won't give me any more. I just need to get through the weekend to wean myself off."

"Trainers? You a jock?" Willie asked.

"Cross-country," Wes said. "Bill was helping me, but he's gone."

"Yeah, I heard about Bill. Tough break. He's a good guy." Pausing for a second, Willie finally said, "You got a car?"

"Yes."

"Tell you what. Be back here at eight tonight, and we will see what we can do."

"Can I at least buy a couple now?"

"Anxious, aren't you," Willie added as the other guys laughed. "Don't push your luck."

The guy Wes had been talking to earlier escorted Wes to the side door, and just before Wes left, the guy gave him a small envelope with two pills in it. "Don't be late," he said.

Wes wandered back into The Library at eight as he had been told. He felt better since he took the pills, but he knew it was only a matter of time before he would be craving more.

Willie was still sitting in the corner with his group, but there were some girls hanging around too.

As Wes moved toward Willie's table, the guy stepped in and stopped him. *He must be the bodyguard or the guardian of the gate,* Wes thought. The guy motioned for Wes to follow him out the side door.

Once they got outside, the guy asked, "You bring your wheels?"

Wes nodded.

"Good. You need to run an errand for Willie to see if you can be trusted. You need to drive those two guys over there sitting on the wall to make a pickup."

"Pick up what?" Wes asked suspiciously.

"Let's just pretend those two pills I gave you were the last two happy pills we had. Does that help?"

Wes nodded. "They'll tell you where to go," the guy said as he turned to reenter the building. Calling back to Wes, he added, "Don't mess it up, and don't take all night."

Wes didn't like the looks of the situation, but if that's what it took to keep from getting sick again and to wean himself, he would do it. *It will be a quick errand, and I only need about a week's worth of pills,* he thought. He got his car and picked up the two guys who didn't look like students. They were big black guys with black sweatshirts. They told him to go to a 7-11 on the Central Highway. When they got there, they told him to park on the side of the building with the car facing toward the highway.

As they climbed out of Wes's car, he asked what they were doing.

"Relax, homeboy. We just gotta pick up a shipment," they said with a laugh. "Leave the car running, and we'll be right back." They disappeared around the corner. There was not much light behind the building, and Wes couldn't see around the corner.

Wes shook his head and felt the shakes returning. *What a mess. But it doesn't matter. By this time next week, I'll be off this stuff.*

He heard several loud bangs, and his two passengers sprinted toward the car and jumped in. "Go, go, go," they screamed.

Wes started to pull away. "What happened?"

"Faster," they screamed. "Drive faster before we get shot."

That was when Wes realized the bangs were gunshots. "Oh, no." He floored the gas pedal.

The two guys were screaming and cussing at the top of their lungs. "A setup, a setup," they kept saying.

They hadn't gone two blocks back toward Clemson when two police cars made a U-turn and came after them.

The guys yelled, "Faster. Turn here."

Wes panicked and did what he was told. *Maybe they aren't after us,* he thought. He rounded a curve, and a police car was blocking their getaway. As Wes hit the brakes, the other two guys got out of the car and ran.

Oh no. If Wes thought his year up to that point had been bad, it was about to get a whole lot worse.

Wes was promptly arrested and taken to jail where he was questioned by a detective in a small, windowless holding room. He was told that they had been tracking Willie for months, trying to catch him red-handed. The spot he drove the two other guys to was a regular drug drop, and the police had been staking it out for a couple of weeks in hopes of catching Willie in person. They weren't going to move on his friends that night since Willie wasn't with them, but his buddies made the mistake of shooting when they spotted the police watching them. One of the officers had been hit, and the detective told Wes that he better start praying that the officer pulled through—or the charges would get a whole lot worse.

Wes tried to explain that he had no idea what was happening. He told the detective the whole story about hurting his ankle, getting hooked on the painkillers, and Bill getting fired. He just needed a few more to wean himself off. That's all he was after. He had never met Willie before that day, and he only went because he was desperate. "I swear it. Please believe me, Officer. What's going to happen?"

The detective told him he was facing several drug charges and was an accomplice to shooting an officer. His car would be confiscated and was the property of the county since it was used in the commission of a drug crime. "It doesn't look good. You better answer all the questions honestly."

They read him his rights, but Wes said he had nothing to hide and continued to answer all their questions. "Absolutely," Wes answered quickly. "Anything to get out of here."

"You won't be going anywhere for a while."

Wes was escorted to a cell and spent the longest night of his life there. The jitters and nausea quickly returned, and he began to vomit. He alternated between lying on the bed in a ball crying in agony and fear and hunched over the toilet. He kept thinking about facing his coach. He would surely be off the team now.

What am I going to do? What am I going to do? Dear God, please help me. Please.

After surviving the sleepless night, Wes found out the officer had died. He would be charged as an accomplice to murder. He slumped on the table and sobbed. "I didn't know. I didn't know," he said.

To make matters worse, the detectives could not find anyone who had seen him in The Library. His two accomplices had been caught after a short chase and said Wes paid them to go to the pickup.

"No, no, no. Willie made me go," Wes cried as the officer left.

Coach Fields came by later that day and asked Wes how in the world it had happened.

Wes sobbed and told him he was so sorry. He was just trying to heal to get back to running so he wouldn't lose his scholarship. Coach tried to reassure him and told him he would make sure he got a good public defender. Running was the least of his worries now.

Wes quickly slipped into despair like he had never known. His running career was over. School was gone, his mom was gone, and his father could care less. His life was over.

I guess he was right all along. I am worthless. It took almost a week to completely detox from the hydrocodone in his system. Very little sleep and not being able to keep any food down had left him a physical and mental wreck. The public defenders tried to get him to perk up, but he was inconsolable.

"It's all over," he kept muttering. "All over."

Wes was denied bond, and he spent the next six months locked up in the county jail. The trial lasted only a few days, and his public defenders advised him to agree to the plea bargain the prosecution was offering. He would plead guilty to lesser charges of conspiracy to purchase drugs and accomplice to manslaughter. Even though the police had been trying to catch Willie in a sting for months, there were no witnesses to corroborate Wes's story.

"It's the best we can hope for," the lawyers said. "An officer lost his life, and the family wants justice."

The only people present for him at the sentencing were Coach Fields, Coach Owings, Kathy, and his pastor. They testified as character witnesses for Wes.

Wes begged for mercy when it was his turn to speak and said he was so sorry. He tried to explain that he was just in the wrong place at the wrong time, and he meant no harm. The detective's family was undeterred and asked for the stiffest sentence possible.

When his sentence of six years was announced, Wes's legs gave away. His lawyers had to support him. It might as well have been the death penalty as far as he was concerned. He sat down slowly, rested his head on the table, and began to sob quietly.

Why, God? Why?

CHAPTER 8

LIFE OR DEATH

I mmediately after the trial, the Department of Corrections drove Wes to the South Carolina medium-security prison on the outskirts of McCormick. The forty-five-minute drive down State Highway 28 would take almost six years of his life and very nearly all of it. Wearing his orange, county-issued jumpsuit, he was shackled in his seat on one side of the van. Shackled on the other side was twenty-five-year-old Jamere Watts, who had been sentenced for the second time for possession of meth within one mile of a school and for breaking and entering.

"Yo, man, you really kill somebody?" the young man said to Wes.

"No," Wes replied quietly as he stared at the floor.

Bursting out in laughter, his van mate said, "Heard that before, dude. Me too. Me too. They call me Hundred Watts or just Watts. Did I hear your name is Wes?"

"Yes." Wes continued to stare uncomfortably at the floor.

"Let me tell you about the McMarriott, man, where we're headed. I spent two years there a while back. It's not your regular white folks' resort. You better watch your back, man, if you know what I mean. There are two groups in there—the Freaks and the Boyz. Unless you got special skills, like me, you better get in with one of those two or you ain't gonna survive. You know what I mean? Me, I got connections on the outside to the meth factory, so I can keep the dudes happy. Everybody likes that. No problem. Keeps everybody mellowed out. So you better have something both sides want or get ready to roll over for the Boyz. Young fresh boy like you gonna be in demand to the Boyz on the inside. And the Freaks, they ain't gonna pick you. Not yet anyway."

And that's how the forty-five-minute ride went—a free speech on life and survival on the inside that would have made little sense to Wes even if he had been listening. Wes bounced from feelings of utter self-loathing and anger over what had happened to fear over what lay ahead as told by his new friend Watts. He still couldn't believe how the trial turned out. He totally expected probation based on his lack of a record. Wrong place at the wrong time—that's all it was. He had no idea what was going down. He kept trying to tell everyone that, but no one would listen, especially the family of the poor guy who got shot. All they wanted was vengeance.

When they finally got to the prison, they took the two new prisoners to an admitting area where their pictures were taken for ID cards. Then, one after the other, they went into a shower area where they were strip-searched and sprayed for parasites. While the two young guards on duty watched Wes go through this degrading process, they laughed to each other as they wagered a bet.

"Two weeks," one said.

"No way he lasts that long," the other one said. "They'll get to him before then. You're gonna have some close friends in here, boy."

Wes thought about the words of his grandmother from many years ago that God had a plan for his life, and he would do great things. *Sure,* he thought. *Great plan this is.* She had died when he was six years old, but her words would surface periodically, usually after his father had told him the opposite. Wes had always struggled to believe her as the events of his young life unfolded but never more so than now. As bad as he hated being alone through this ordeal, he was very thankful that his grandmother and his mom were not alive to see this.

It would kill them, he thought as the thoughts washed over him like the cold shower water.

Wes wanted to burst out crying, but he knew he could never show any weakness in prison to anyone—no matter how bad it got. After his shower, the prison guards gave him a lecture on the prison rules: when to eat, when to turn out the lights, and when to go outside to the recreation yard. Wes was assigned a job in the kitchen that would start at six the following morning. Then, they gave him a new orange prison jumpsuit and escorted him to his cell. Going through the cell block was like being in a strip club. Half the prisoners in their cells started whistling and calling out to him as they got up to see the new blood.

"Hey, boy, come here. Let me see what you got," said one.

"Nice body, white boy," said another. "I'll be your daddy."

On and on it went, getting worse as they walked along. There were three floors with cells on each side and a twenty-foot open space in between that extended down to the first floor. All the guards did was smile and laugh at the show. They seemed to enjoy the parade as the catcalls echoed off the walls. Finally, they arrived at Wes's new eight-by-eight home: a single bed on one side, sink in the far corner, and toilet in the other corner. There would be no privacy in this drab, gray environment. As if the grayness that surrounded him was contagious, the reality of his new dismal existence began to sink into his soul. He stared at the sad walls, let out a long sigh, and sat down on the bed. *How in the world did I get here?*

As the guard shut the door, he chuckled and said, "Watch yourself, kid."

The only small positive Wes could think of was that at least he had a cell by himself. At least he would be safe in his cell from the crazies on the outside. *God in heaven, if you're up there, please, please help me. Get me out of here.* He wanted to scream and cry so bad, but he knew he couldn't show any emotion. He felt utterly hopeless and without a friend in the world.

In the weeks ahead, Kathy would try to visit him, but he refused her visits. Instead, Wes sent her a message to sell whatever few things of his that his mother had left at her place and to leave him alone. It was just too painful for him to have contact with the outside world. As far as he was concerned, the outside world did not exist anymore. It was just as well since no one else tried to contact him. Forgotten by the world and in deep despair, Wes tried to prepare himself for what lay ahead.

The next morning at six o'clock sharp, he was escorted to the wash area of the kitchen and introduced to Mike, the prisoner in charge of cleanup. Mike was a heavyset, middle-aged white guy with a bushy black beard and bushier full head of black hair that made him look like a pirate. "New guys start out washing dishes, kid. No other choices. Do your job, keep up, and we'll get along. Drag your behind, and I'll turn you over to some of these Fruit Loops for an attitude adjustment. Got it."

Wes nodded.

"What you in for?" Mike asked. On the inside, it seemed like this always was the second question after being asked his name. It was as if on the inside, one's crime became part of his name. Last names were no longer necessary.

Wes hesitated; he still wasn't comfortable admitting what he had been convicted of. He had difficulty attaching the words, as if the two could not possibly be compatible. It was a label he just didn't want anything to do with. The first thing he wanted to say initially was that it was a big mistake. He didn't do anything. Wrong place, right time. After hesitating, he quietly said, "Accomplice to manslaughter."

With a smile, Mike said, "Let me guess, you didn't have anything to do with it. Me too. I sure didn't mean to shoot my woman's boyfriend, but I sure meant to pistol-whip that lying female." He burst out laughing as he walked off. "Get to work, kid," he said as he threw his towel over his shoulder and glanced back at his new charge.

So every morning at six, Wes was escorted to the dining hall where he and the other workers were allowed to eat quickly before the other inmates. He then reported to his new job and stood over the deep, shiny sink and cleaned the oversize pots and pans from breakfast with a scrub brush and dishrags. They were then hung up to dry. The small pans and cooking utensils were washed in another sink. Watts was put in charge of that sink. The inmates used plastic plates, cups, and utensils and were not given anything that could be turned into a weapon. The washing mainly consisted of the items used to prepare the food and the trays it was placed on for delivery to the inmates.

Wes and Watts were separated from the other areas by a strong steel-wire partition, but they could still see and hear what was going on in other parts of the kitchen. The guard assigned to the kitchen was an older white man named Bill. He was a short, heavyset fellow with thin, gray hair who looked like he should be guarding cars instead of violent prisoners. He probably would not be much good in a serious fight, but at least he was nice. Wes's new mealtime routine was to eat quickly and then get to his assignment with Watts. Watts never failed to entertain; he talked constantly, which at least took the edge off the boredom.

The first weeks went by pretty much the same without any major incidents. Wes was wary of not being caught anywhere alone and getting back to his cell as quick as he could each day. Being one of the new inmates, he got a lot of looks as if he was being sized up. Or maybe it was to intimidate him. There still were a lot of catcalls and not-so-innocent sexual comments. He kept to himself and didn't respond to any of the comments thrown his way, and he definitely avoided eye contact. His most nervous time was the shower. It was a community shower with ten nozzles along one wall—the worst kind in front of this group of malfeasants. With all his glory showing to the world, Wes made quick business in there and made sure there were always plenty of other people around. There were always two guards posted outside the entrance to the shower, which was not close enough as far as Wes was concerned. Showers were required at least once a week, and at first, that was all Wes wanted.

The other area he wasn't sure about was the recreation area. It was an open area about half the size of a football field—not a lot of room for several hundred angry, incarcerated men. There were some bleachers in one corner, a basketball goal in another, and free weights in the third. The last corner was a question. There always seemed to be a group of about twenty or so black men and a few white men in that last corner, always standing in a tight group. They huddled together in conversation and looked sinister. Wes tried not to stare, but he wasn't sure what was going on over there.

The bleachers in the first corner had some of the biggest, toughest, most muscular guys in the place. The odd group included about thirty black, white, and Hispanic men. Wes would later learn that they were the Freaks, and the evil-looking guys in the last corner were the Boyz. Wes just stayed to himself and walked circles in the middle of the compound, never stopping, and never making eye contact. He always stayed at arm's length from the other inmates. His goal was to be as invisible as possible.

During this early time, Wes was filled with self-hate and anger. He thought that if he could get out and run, he could go for days—or until he dropped dead in his tracks. As far as he was concerned, that would be fine too. He had reached the point where he really didn't care if he lived or died. He had been deep in the well when his father berated him, but those days were nothing compared to what was going on in his head now. At least he had a future then, and there was a light at the top of the well, even if he would not have admitted it. But it didn't matter now. The well was sealed with no light in sight. No hope. Even if he survived this purgatory, what kind of a future could he have as an ex-convict? He was as low as low could be. Wes wasn't suicidal yet, but the thought had crossed his mind. He wasn't going to pick a fight to end it, but he knew that if anybody touched him, he was ready to fight to the end. To him, his life was over anyway.

Was it more a form of self-punishment or self-preservation? Was he berating himself further to add to the punishment he felt like he deserved, as if trying to prove his father right? Or was he steeling his resolve to survive in this new cruel existence he had been thrust into? At this point, a thin line separated the two—and it would be hard to say what his real motivation was. Did he really want to live or die? He was about to find out.

While working in the kitchen, Wes had picked up from Watts that the Boyz were a group of violent drug addicts who had no morals or scruples. They would rape, kill, or do whatever it took to satisfy their urge of the moment. They were led by Shadevious, a young, twice-convicted major drug dealer. He went by the nickname Devious, but it was the things he had not been arrested for that built his reputation. He had been known to maim and kill family members of subordinates to teach submission. He had a network inside and out of prison to get whatever he wanted. And he always got whatever or whoever he wanted. He was the fearless, undisputed boss of the Boyz. The guards either turned a blind eye to his exploits as long as no one was killed on their watch or they were willing to accept his payoffs.

Devious had his eye on Wes since he got there. Young, athletic Wes had no connections or protection on the inside. That was the warning everyone had been alluding to since Wes started serving his sentence. Wes learned quickly to avoid Devious, but two months after Wes arrived, he had gotten a little too comfortable with the routine.

On a Saturday evening, he was running behind and was one of the last ones in the shower. He wasn't paying attention as the other guys quickly exited as if on cue while Wes showered off. Devious and one of his henchmen quietly snuck in. Wes turned around to find himself alone and facing his worst nightmare. It was a life-or-death decision. Would he submit to these guys and become one of their stooges and live? Or did he really want to defend himself and unleash all that anger and self-hate, which might save his life? These guys were bigger, meaner fighting machines and knew how to bend people to their wills. Wes had about thirty seconds to make a decision that would either end his short life or define the rest of it.

"On your knees, boy," a muscular white guy with a Mohawk said as Devious dropped his pants.

Wes knew it was futile to call for help, and he didn't like the other two choices he had: give in or fight. He wasn't sure if he wanted to live or die, but he did know he was not going to go to his knees without a fight. Slowly, Wes bent over and put his hands on his knees as he gathered himself and quickly tried to come up with a plan. If he could just get past these two, he might have a chance to reach the exit.

Devious looked at his assistant and laughingly said, "That's a good boy."

As the two thugs shared a laugh, Wes swiftly kicked the bodyguard in the groin and bolted for the exit. His decision hinged on making it to the exit before either of the two bad guys did. It would have worked too, but as he tried to make the ninety-degree turn for the exit, he slipped and fell on the wet floor. The thug got to him first and kicked him in the gut. Wes quickly jumped to his feet and, not being a fighter, unleashed all his anger in a burst of fury on the two men. He flailed, kicked, and yelled for all he had. A few punches made their mark, but for the most part, it was a futile effort. The other two guys had been there before and knew what to do. When Wes's explosion began to subside, they both launched into him. It only took several punches to put him on the floor. The two bigger guys kicked him in the ribs and head continuously as Wes yelled for dear life.

The two guards outside the door—who had been paid off to turn their heads for ten minutes—soon had heard enough. They didn't want other guards to come see what the ruckus was about and see them doing nothing. They ran into the shower where Wes was getting pummeled unmercifully on the floor. His blood mixed freely with the water on the floor and flowed in a steady, life-draining trickle toward the shower drain. The guards told the thugs to get out and called the infirmary for help.

Wes was unconscious but alive.

CHAPTER 9

GUARDIAN ANGELS

Wes could barely open one eye as he struggled to regain consciousness. He became immediately aware of the splitting pain in his head and the pain in his chest as he tried to breathe. He tried to talk, but the medicine that he had been given for pain made him slur his words.

When the medical personnel realized he was coming around, they rushed over to check on him. They explained that he had been brought to Self Memorial Hospital in Greenwood, and he needed to try to stay as still as possible. He had a concussion, three broken ribs, a punctured lung, a bruised spleen, and a broken right hand. His left wrist was handcuffed to the bed rail.

"What happened?" he stammered.

"You were in a fight at the prison," the nurse replied.

"Oh," was all he could mouth as he faded off to sleep again.

Over the ensuing days, Wes learned that he would be in the hospital for at least a week to make sure his head injury and spleen were healing okay. The headaches slowly subsided along with his swollen right eye. It hurt to breathe deeply, and Wes had to take short, rapid breaths, which kept him tired and feeling like he was constantly fighting to catch his breath. He knew his physical injuries would heal, but the psychological damage was even worse.

Officials from the jail had come to interview him and told him that the other two inmates said Wes had started the fight. Without other witnesses, there was not a lot that could be done. The two thugs were given ten days in solitary confinement for fighting—a slap on the wrist in other words. When Wes was cleared to return to the prison, he would be given the same amount of time in solitary confinement, more for his own protection than anything else. He asked if it would be possible to be transferred to another facility.

"This stuff happens all the time, kid. Learn to get along," he was told.

Wes knew what that meant. Give in or give out. He was terrified of what he might have to face on his return, and he knew this wouldn't be the end of it. Begging the doctors to keep him longer did no good. No possibility, he was told. Not much sympathy for a convict who gets in a fight. But how could he defend himself with a broken hand?

The day arrived too quickly for Wes to be discharged back to the McMarriott. He still had a black eye, his ribs were still bruised, and he had a cast on his right hand. As he was escorted to solitary confinement, he heard the same old catcalls. However, this time they were filled with dire warnings.

"Better enjoy your vacation in solitary, homeboy. Your days are numbered."

"Nice move, tough guy. They'll be waiting for you."

Wes did his best to ignore them, but he knew they were right. Those kinds of guys would be out for revenge, and they wouldn't waste time getting it. What in the world would he do? Wes had no friends inside, and the authorities could care less. He felt totally abandoned. He had made the choice to live, and now it looked like that might not work out. On his last night in solitary, he got down on his knees, clasped his hands, and emptied his heart.

His despair had reached the very bottom. He had nowhere else to turn, and he finally realized it.

The tears slowly trickled down his face and he started to pray. "Dear God in heaven, please help me. I've always tried to do right, but I messed up. I know it. I never should have been in that car trying to get more drugs. It was all my fault. There's nobody to blame but me. I'm so sorry that detective died. So sorry. When I got here, I didn't care if I lived or died, but I want to live. I don't know what your plan is, God, but I'm going to believe my grandmother. Somehow, even in this mess, you do have a good plan for me. Please help me—and protect me—when I get out of here tomorrow. I'm sorry. Thank you."

Wes didn't sleep a wink that night. He knew he would never give in to those deviants. He would fight. He might die or end up in the hospital again, but he would be strong. He wasn't sure what he was feeling. It wasn't confidence, that was for sure, but a steely resolve that he would be true to himself if nothing else. He had made wrong choices in the past, but he was determined to make the right ones from now on. If he died, he would die trying to be a better person.

When morning came around, the guard came for him before breakfast. "Wes, it's Bill."

Wes squinted at the bright light shining from the hallway into his darkened cell. "I'm going to try to look out for you, but be careful out there. Hopefully, Preacher will contact you today. Listen to what he has to say."

It was the first kindness that had been shown him since his arrival. Wes nodded and tried to process the kindly, older guard's instructions. *Who is Preacher?*

Since he had a cast on his lower arm, Wes was given a break for a few days from kitchen duty. He went through the meal line at breakfast with the other inmates, got his tray, and picked a table by himself in the middle of the room. He felt all the eyes on him, and he heard the giggles as he walked by. Wes knew nothing would happen in the lunchroom in front of everybody, so he kept his eyes on his plate.

After a few minutes, he heard a hush come over the room. Wes looked up.

Devious and his henchmen were standing directly in front of him. Without a word, they sat down across from him and stared Wes down for several minutes as if they would attack at any second. It was the fierce lion pausing before pouncing on his prey. To his credit, Wes did not flinch. He stared right back, and when they finally started eating, he continued to eat without taking his eyes off Devious. He finished as quickly as he could, exited the lunchroom, and got to his cell. He was safe for the moment.

Exercise time came too soon, and all the inmates were released into the open compound. That was the time Wes feared most; anything could happen out there in that jungle of testosterone. Maybe if he saw it coming, he could run. At least he felt like he could outrun any of these guys, but space was limited in the rec area. Wes decided he would go to the middle of the compound and just keep moving in a circle. He hadn't been there long when three huge guys appeared in his path—two black and one white. Their arms were as big around as Wes's thighs. He stopped in his tracks and glanced around for an exit. With no handy outlet available, he stepped back and drew his right arm back.

This is it. He glanced nervously at the three behemoths in his path. He didn't recognize them as belonging to Devious's Boyz, but they didn't look particularly friendly either. *Hopefully, the guards are watching*, Wes thought.

"Relax, dude," the white guy finally said. "We're your guardian angels. Preacher wants to see you." He pointed to the corner bleachers where the Freaks hung out.

The two black guys led the way, and the white guy walked beside him as Wes hesitantly followed. Wes was very suspicious of what might happen, but Bill had mentioned Preacher that morning. Wes's heart raced, and his eyes darted about, still waiting for the assault to come at any moment.

When they got to the corner, the crowd parted. He was escorted to a thin, middle-aged black man with salt-and-pepper hair and a thin beard who was sitting on the front row of the bench. He motioned for Wes to take a seat beside him. With his eyes darting about for danger like a ball in a pinball machine, Wes was on high alert.

"I'm fine," Wes quickly replied.

"Wes, you're safe. Relax. Nobody will hurt you here."

Wes was still very cautious and stood his ground as the man stood up.

"They call me Preacher. Think of me as Peter at the Pearly Gates. I'm not an angel—just the doorman trying to show folks the right path to take to get back on track. Problem is most people 'round here wouldn't have a clue. All they're interested in is surviving and some instant 'feel good.' I've been watching you, and I don't think you're like those guys." He motioned toward the Boyz corner. "I think you've got potential."

Wes glanced around warily as the older fellow said, "Potential to be saved that is. You just need to hear the right message. You might have heard we were Freaks. That's true—Jesus Freaks. Everybody over here has messed up bad, but what separates us from the rest of the guys in here is that we know it—and we want to do better. By the grace of God, we have been saved. We are trying to make things right and not make the same mistakes again. You understand what I'm saying? You interested?"

Wes didn't know if this was the answer to his prayer or somebody else with an agenda. All he could think of to say was,

"So, why did you wait till I was almost killed?" It kind of ticked him off if what the guy was saying was true, and he had let those guys almost kill him or rape him or both before reaching out to him. *Why now?*

Preacher laughed a deep hearty laugh and said, "Had to test you, my boy. A lot of the guys who come through here will either say anything to make their life easier or will take the position for any of those Boyz over there to save their skin. You were willing to fight for your life. That means something. Means you're pretty solid in here." He pointed to his heart. "I'm sorry you got hurt, but you're safe now. My guys will look after you. Escort you to the shower and everywhere else."

"What guys? And why? And what do you expect from me?" Wes was still peeved that they had not reached out to him earlier.

Pointing over to the monsters lifting weights, Preacher smiled and said, "Those big old angels over there. Like I said, I think you've got potential. I think God has a good plan for you. And I don't expect anything. Would hope I've stirred up your curiosity enough to listen to God's Word now and then. That's all. How do those answers sound?"

Wes nodded and looked around in amazement. *Is this guy telling the truth? Why did he pick me? And why now?*

"And by the way, Big Frank and Wolf will be your new neighbors." Preacher pointed to two of the big guys that had escorted Wes over to Preacher. "Seems a cell just opened up in between theirs, and the warden thought you might like to have it."

Could this really be the answer to his prayer from the night before? Thoughts raced through Wes's mind as he tried to comprehend this latest turn of events. He had prayed before, especially when his father was throwing a fit, but he had never seen results—at least not immediate results like this.

If this is true, God, then thank you. Thank you so much.

CHAPTER 10

PREACHER

In the days and months ahead, Wes felt like a celebrity, but he dared not show it. Whenever his cell door opened, one of his new friends was there. It didn't matter where he was headed—the kitchen, shower, break area, mealtime—they were always there. He thanked God several times a day for them. He felt so much better having them around, but Wes was still on his guard. Things might still go bad, and the Boyz might try something. There were plenty of stares and insults thrown his way, but as time went on, he was able to relax a little more. The Boyz would not dare attack the Freaks, it seemed. Not yet anyway.

Whenever they were released into the recreation area, Wes always headed to Preacher's corner. Initially, it was for protection more than anything else. Preacher was always there talking. He never stopped. Wes thought it was interesting that Preacher always had a way of working the conversation back around to religion. He figured that's where he got his nickname. One day on the way to the recreation area, Wes asked Big Frank how Preacher got his nickname and what he was in for.

"Oh, I best leave that story to him. Don't worry though; it's coming eventually." Big Frank chuckled as they walked along.

Wes furrowed his brow and glanced at Wolf.

The burly escorts let out a loud laugh. Wes thought Wolf's name was appropriate. He was a short, stocky, muscle-bound white guy with a mane of long, golden blond hair. With his ever-present white headband and pointed nose and ears, he looked just like a wolf.

The other Freaks were an odd mixture of men. That's originally where Wes thought their name originated. Some were giant muscle men, including Big Frank, Wolf, Stick, Hulk, and Tiny. Some of the older guys, like Dean, Walt, and Scott, looked like they couldn't hurt a flea. Wes couldn't understand a few of the Hispanics, like Diego and Luis. A few other young guys, looked like they needed protection from the vultures on the other side of the yard too.

Preacher paid attention to all the guys who hung around him, but Wes felt like he got extra attention. Preacher always had something to say to him. Initially, Wes was on guard about Preacher's motives, but his guard came down as he learned he had nothing to fear on that side of the yard. Eventually he would learn Preacher's ultimate motive.

Preacher really knew the Bible too. He could quote verses off the top of his head or launch into an impromptu devotional. Whatever the situation dictated, he was prepared. When Wes got to the yard, Preacher might be talking to a small group or an individual, and Wes knew to give them space. Other days, he would be launching into a devotional to the whole group. He was always ready. He was part counselor, part therapist, and all minister.

Wes watched him in awe as the days went by. He had heard ministers preach, but this guy was special. Wes had been to church with his mom and had heard his grandmother's words. He had tried to listen in church, but he never understood much of what was being said. His father had never let him go back to youth group activities on Sunday nights, so he never had really been around the young religious nerds at his church. They generally weren't in the "cool" group at school either. Wes's religious training had been limited.

Wes had basically looked at God as some tough Father in the sky who was waiting for him to mess up so he could punish him—just like his earthly father did. Since he usually didn't feel like he had done anything wrong to receive his father's wrath, Wes came to feel like when something went wrong that he must have done something wrong. God was punishing him. Reward and retribution—plain and simple. Old Testament theology. *Bad things happened, so I must deserve it.* It was pretty twisted—but not when you had experienced it for your whole life. It has been said that humans base their perceptions of how God works on their relationships with their earthly fathers. Loving earthly father? Then our Heavenly Father must be a loving Father. Strict judgmental earthly father? Then our Heavenly Father must be the same. This definitely was true of Wes.

At first, Preacher chitchatted with Wes about how he was healing and his kitchen job. Wes's ribs were healed, but he still had his cast on his hand. He had been shifted from dishwashing to loading the wet pans in the drying racks after they had been washed. Big Frank and several of the other Freaks worked in this area, which was a relief. Wes felt like maybe those guys were giving Preacher feedback about how he was doing since Preacher seemed to know his mood on any given day. And his mood definitely could change from day to day. Prison does that to a person. One minute, you can be coping with incarceration, and then the next minute, the stark reality of the situation smacks you in the face—the realization that along with your sentence, your life is ticking away. Wes had plenty of those moments in his first year at the McMarriott. On bad days, Preacher tried to calm him and lift his spirits. On good days, he seized his chance and tried to slide his message in.

"You grow up in a church?" Preacher asked one day as they sat alone under a sunny October sky. It had been slightly over a year since Wes arrived at the McMarriott.

"Kinda. I went with my mom on Sundays. I tried to listen, but I didn't really understand," Wes replied.

"Yeah, me too," Preacher replied. "It's hard to grab at that age. I think most of the time the guys behind the pulpit make it harder than they have to. Not that they mean to. They get paid to deliver a message, so they have to use a lot of words to fill up a time slot. They could probably get their point across with a lot less words. Know what I mean?"

"Yeah." Wes smiled.

Preacher laughed and said, "So, it's not their fault. They're trying to make a living and spread the gospel, but it's really not that hard or deep. Actually, it's hard to accept in its simplicity. Somebody does something really big for you, and then you want to do something to earn it and pay them back. But the gospel doesn't work that way. We are freely given a gift, and all we have to do is accept it. It's called grace. We tough guys don't like to talk about it. I don't know why we get so embarrassed. You would think once we get it, we'd want to shout it from the rooftops and in the streets. That's really all I'm trying to do here. I'm just trying to get through to as many of these guys as I can. The Good Lord has done so much for me, and I just want to spread that around. You understand?"

"Got it," Wes said as he wondered how this guy could be thanking God for being in this cesspool. *He must have had too many licks to the head.*

The bell sounded for them to return to their cells.

"Good," Preacher said. "Here's your homework. You got that Gideon Bible in your cell, right?"

Wes nodded.

"Go to Romans in the New Testament and start looking at chapter 8, okay?"

"Okay," Wes said.

The next day started out just like most all the others for Wes. Alarm at six o'clock and then a quick breakfast before his shift in the kitchen. Late in the afternoon was his time in the recreation area that he looked forward to.

Big Frank and Stick, another NFL-sized black man with a huge Afro, were his escorts on this bright sunny Tuesday in October. There was a slight bottleneck as they left the building and entered the yard. At the same time Wes stepped to go around the guy in front of him, the guy stepped into Wes's path. It was all an accident of bad timing. Wes bumped into him, immediately apologized, and stepped back. The guy was one of the Boyz, but Wes did not recognize him in time. The guy wheeled on Wes and shoved him down in a flash. Big Frank and Stick jumped between the two instantly and held the guy at arm's length. The guards at the door jumped in to make sure things didn't get out of hand and told everyone to move on. Some insults and warnings were thrown at Wes, and that was the end of it. Such was the reality of Wes's existence.

As Wes reached Preacher's corner, he glanced at Preacher, and they both shook their heads in disbelief. Preacher was still staring in the direction from where Wes, Frank, and Stick had come to make sure everything had settled down. When he was satisfied, he turned and sat down with Wes.

Wes said, "I've got a question. So how have you guys kept from killing each other over the years? There seems to be so much bad blood."

Preacher looked down and thought for a second. "Good question. There have been plenty of chances over the years. The short answer is somewhat peaceful coexistence. As a Christian, I know that killing is wrong, and I want with all my heart to spread the gospel, but I can't do that if we are dead. So we have to pray for God's protection and guidance, and we will defend ourselves if we are attacked. Those guys over there have no conscience or morals. They'll do whatever it takes to satisfy their latest need or desire. And Devious … well, let's just say his mama sure named him right. All I can do is pray for them and hope to reach one or two of them along the way, but that's doubtful. But I'll go after anybody else that has potential. Like you, my man." Preacher smiled at Wes and patted him on the back.

Wes smiled slightly and said, "But it looks like they get away with so much—drugs and rape—is there nothing that can be done?"

"It's in the Lord's hands. We could report everything we see, but that would just lead to war and paybacks, and that won't help any of us. As long as they keep it in their sick little circle, and it keeps them under control … 'Vengeance is mine,' sayeth the Lord.'"

After a few minutes of staring off into space, Preacher finally said, "So did you look at Romans 8?"

"A little," Wes replied.

"A little? Well, it's a start," Preacher said with a grin. "Go back tonight and look at it hard. One verse at a time and think about it."

Wes looked down at the dirt and said, "I don't know. I … I appreciate all you've done for me, but I'm just not sure."

Preacher quickly said, "Not sure about what?"

"I just think God's got bigger fish to fry than me. I'm pretty sure after the things I've done and what I've become that it's too—"

"Too what? Too late?" Preacher said. "You think you're the only person in here who feels that way? Or the only person in South Carolina? Or the United States? Or the world? You go back and read chapter 8 closer, and we'll talk more. Okay?"

"All right," Wes mumbled.

Every day for the next month, Preacher would ask Wes if he had read Romans chapter 8.

Wes would say, "A little," or he'd nod.

Every day, Preacher would say, "Read it again. Read it closer. And memorize that first verse and that last verse in chapter 8. They're the most important ones. You believe them, and everything in between will fall into place. Just like your first breath and your last. They're the main ones. If you trust everything in between to Him, it will be okay."

"You got 'em memorized?" Preacher would ask each day.

"Getting there," Wes would reply with a grin.

"You better." Preacher pointed a finger at Wes. "Your test is coming."

As the days went by, Preacher kept quoting certain Bible verses and talking about them. Wes began to look at Romans 8 a little closer. He listened with interest one day as Preacher quoted Romans 8:32. *What did it mean that God gave up His Son for us?*

Preacher said, "God was a just and righteous God who demanded payment for sin—all sin. No matter how big the sin—whether it be murder, lying on your income tax, rape, cheating on your homework, or stealing a pack of gum—all of them in the same bag. There's no 'big' sins and no 'little' sins. Just sin. Since we all sin, both prisoners and free folks, and fall short, how could we ever pay for that sin?

"God loves us so much," Preacher continued, "that he sent His Son, His *only* Son, to die for all of our sins—past, present, and future. Everybody's. Yours and even theirs." He pointed across the yard to the Boyz. "He did it one time for the past, present, and future. All we have to do is believe it and trust him. That's it. Nothing else. There is not one thing we can do to earn it. Just believe and trust. Sleep on that one, guys."

That one hit a nerve with Wes. Ever since he had been convicted, he had wondered sometimes if that meant he could not go to heaven. But that was not what Preacher was saying. Trust and believe. Preacher had Wes's full attention now.

Wes went back to his cell and looked a little closer at Romans chapter 8. The next day, Preacher asked Wes what he thought about what he had said the day before.

"Interesting," Wes replied. "So, maybe there is a little hope."

"Yeah. There is a lot of hope, my boy." Preacher smiled and gave Wes a little push. "Sit down. Let me tell you about a devotional I read about a guy who attended an Easter sunrise service at the edge of the Grand Canyon. Seems this guy had been really struggling with the mistakes in his life and how he could ever deserve God's love. The preacher at that sunrise service that day pointed out over that big, big valley that you could barely see the bottom of or the other side. He told those folks, as the sun came up on that Easter Sunday, that no matter how wide and deep that beautiful place was, that God loved them more than that. No matter what they had done, His love for them would overflow that canyon. The guy said right then and there it finally sank in: God loves us no matter what. The man cried like a baby. Changed him forever. Can you imagine being in that place and having that message preached to you? That's powerful stuff."

Preacher turned to straddle the bench and faced Wes. "So you've been studying Romans a while now. Tell me what the last verse means."

Wes looked down for a second. "I guess it means that God loves us no matter what."

"You *guess*? You *guess*?" Preacher raised his voice. "Boy, there is no guessing in the Good Book. It either says it or it doesn't. So what does it say?"

"Okay," Wes said with a laugh. "It says that God loves us no matter what."

"Good. Now, do you believe it? Yes or no? And remember this, God don't like no fence straddlers. Revelation 3:16 says, 'Because you are lukewarm—neither hot nor cold—I am about to spit you out of my mouth.'"

"I'm trying to," Wes said.

"Listen, Wes. This is the whole key to the Pearly Gates. You either believe it and trust Him or you don't. God don't want try-ers—he wants believers. I know it's tough from where we sit, but you chew on that one for a while, and then you start looking at the verse above it that says, 'In all things we know that God works for the good of those who love him.' You grab onto those two lines, and you hold on with all you got. When you do, you know it's going to be okay. They can lock you up and throw away the key. It don't matter 'cause then you got the key that matters—the eternal key. Okay?"

"Okay," Wes said.

"All right then. You keep working on Romans 8," Preacher said as he stood up.

"Preacher?" Wes asked before he stood up. "So what's your story? What you in for?"

"Now that's a story for another day, my boy. Another day." Preacher smiled and waved his hand in the air as he walked off without looking back.

CHAPTER 11

THE MESSAGE

Wes's life fell into a very familiar routine as it does for most all inmates: up early to eat and then off to his job in the kitchen. His cast had been removed, so it was back to the grind. He was thankful none of the Boyz worked in the kitchen. There were a few Freaks, and he could relax a little and do his job. Watts was ever the entertainer, and he kept Wes amused while they were working.

"So when's your next title fight, big guy? Ali called you yet?" Watts teased. "Seriously, man, I'm glad you okay and Preacher is looking after you."

"Yeah, me too. You ever listen to Preacher?" Wes asked.

"Me? Nah, man," Watts replied. "I ain't got time for that religion stuff. I got to make me some money. M-O-N-E-Y. Too many brothers in here need stuff from the outside that I can get. You understand."

"Yeah." Wes laughed. "Well, I'm sure he'd be glad to have you. He's pretty cool."

The highlight of Wes's day, if there could be such a thing in prison, was his time in the rec yard after lunch. Wes liked listening to Preacher. He made him laugh, and he was interesting to listen to. He usually made time to talk to some of his guys individually, but he also seemed to have a story for whoever would listen. And they weren't just some jive, "running your mouth" kind of stories. Preacher's stories always had a good point. It didn't matter if he had an audience of one or twenty. He was always ready.

And he loved Romans chapter 8. He would quote it all the time. Periodically, he would talk to Wes about different verses from Romans. Wes wasn't sure where it all was headed, but listening to Preacher made him feel better. It helped get his mind off his surroundings for a little while. He liked hearing about the different people Preacher talked about and the way he related their stories to what was going on in his life. Other people who had been through rough times had turned it around.

"You guys ever heard of John Newton?" Preacher asked. He'd wait a minute for a nod or shake of the head and then say, "Come on. Where you been? How about 'Amazing Grace'? John Newton wrote 'Amazing Grace' back in the 1600s. You know what he did for a living before he wrote that song? He was a slave trader. Probably caught our great-great-granddaddies." He would laugh and point to one of his black listeners. "Actually, he was from England, and his father was a slave trader, so he kind of fell into the same work. They were both captains of a slave ship that would make runs to Africa, pick up a cargo of waiting slaves to take back to England, and then sell them at the London slave market at the port. Hard, mean, cruel life. And he was good at it. Eventually, he had his own ship. Doubt he treated his chained passengers too well. Probably lost a few on the trip, but that was to be expected. It was just the cost of doing business. On one trip, they ran into a rough storm—the worst he had ever seen. It looked like they were going down for sure. Just when things were at their worst, old John Newton fell to his knees in his cabin and cried out to God. The God his grandmother had told him about, but he had chosen to ignore. 'Please, God, just get me through this, and I'll be a changed man. I swear it.' Now, I bet God has heard that one a time or two."

Everyone laughed.

"Probably heard it in here too," Preacher said with a laugh as he pointed to the drab, gray walls. "I don't know or understand everything about God, but I know he answered that white man's prayer. He survived that storm. Do you think old John Newton held up his end of the bargain? He sure did. He sold that boat and became a preacher. Few years later, he wrote that song: Amazing grace / how sweet the sound that saved a wretch like me / I once was lost, but now I'm found / Was blind, but now I see." How many people you think he killed or beat or sold into slavery? And now everybody sings his song. I'd say something pretty good ended up coming out of that man's life after he hit the bottom."

Preacher would sit down on his bench, stare way off into the Southern sky, and allow his words to sink in for a little while like barbeque marinade on pork chops. He was just trying to shine a little light into the darkness. He knew what he was doing, and he was doggone good at it.

Lots of days, Preacher would pick somebody out of the Bible and just tell a story about him. He didn't preach in a church preacher kind of way where he was talking down to his listeners and making them feel guilty for not being good Christians. He was just telling a story with a good point. You didn't have to listen. He wanted you to, but he wasn't going to make you. Choice was yours. He was just throwing seeds out on the dusty ground, hoping some fell on fertile soil and took hold. Just like the parable of the sower.

His favorite theme was God's rescue of the lost and how God tended to use lost and broken people to do great things. God saves the lost, and He uses them to further His kingdom. It is a lot like

God's mercy and grace. He doesn't give us the punishments we deserve, and he showers us with blessings we don't deserve.

"God works in mysterious ways they say," Preacher would say, "and one of those mysteries might be you or me. You never know."

At first, Wes had sat off to the side and listened halfheartedly, but as time went on and Preacher paid him more personal attention, he made sure he was at the front of the crowd to hear what Preacher had to say. He still wasn't sure he bought into all this Bible stuff, but he felt like he owed it to God for protecting him since he got out of the hospital. And the best way to do that was to listen to Preacher. Besides, his stories made prison life a little more tolerable and gave him a tad bit of hope. Hope for what? He had no idea. Hope was the most precious commodity inside those walls. It was even more precious than life itself; without hope, a man was dead. And Preacher was giving it out freely. Listening to Preacher definitely made Wes feel better.

Some days, Wes and Preacher just sat on the bench and watched everybody else. On those days, Preacher would quiz Wes about his past. He had won Wes's trust in the months he had known him, and Wes was beginning to open up to Preacher like he never had to anyone else. Wes told him about his father and how he had treated him. "Never have been able to figure that guy out," Wes would say as he shook his head. "I was a good kid too. Made good grades, pretty good in sports, stayed out of trouble. But it never was good enough for him. He was always mad about something. If I had to pick one word to describe him, it would be anger. Man, when he got mad and clenched his jaw and started cussing and throwing things, I thought his teeth would just shatter. Scared me to death. He always told me no wonder I couldn't do things—play football and stuff. I guess he was right. Here I am, and there he is on the outside. I don't guess it really matters anymore; I'll never see him again. Haven't seen him in years since he kicked my mom out. Funny thing—during my trial, I could just imagine him out there saying, 'I told you so.'" Wes kicked the dirt nervously with his right foot as if to dig a hole to bury those thoughts in.

After a little pause, Preacher said, "Never knew my father. Left before I was born. I'm not sure which load is heavier—yours or mine. Never having one or having one that treated you like dirt."

Wes looked up at his friend and continued, "As I got older, I would get mad at my mom sometimes for staying with him. I thought it couldn't be any worse. I think I still hold a grudge against her for that sometimes. But she just did the best she could. Her take on religion would never let her leave. 'Married for life' and all that. Besides, what could she do without an education? We had a house and food just not much of a home. I never saw much love in there. I don't remember him ever saying he loved me or was proud of me. One time when I was playing baseball, I ran down a ball that was hit up the middle to my right when I was playing second. Well, I didn't know he had come to get me for supper and saw that play. I can still see him saying that was a pretty good stop I made. I guess I remember it so well 'cause there was so little of that kind of positive encouragement from him." Wes paused and kicked at the ground some more. "I have to say though that it wasn't all completely bad. He did take me hunting and fishing. I think that was when he was the most relaxed and most normal. I do love the outdoors because of that. I just had to be real careful not to set him off during those times. It could go bad real quick. I think that's why I have a pretty good sense of reading people's faces and expressions to know when they're fixing to go off. Makes you kinda sensitive to that kind of thing."

If listening is what makes a therapist good, then Preacher was a really good therapist. He genuinely cared about his guys. When you have that much time on your hands like prison provides you, you are generally either a good listener or a good talker, whether it's talking to yourself or someone else. Preacher had mastered it. He also seemed to know a lot about Wes's running career—short as it was—and his trial.

Wes didn't care to talk about either of those topics.

On a day in March, Preacher asked a small group of his guys if any of them knew Passover was the next Sunday.

They all just stared at him.

"Know what that is?" he asked.

"Is that when Jesus went to Jerusalem for the last time?" one of them ventured.

Preacher shook his head. "Yeah, but do you know how it started—what it means?"

They all looked down as if they were scared he would call on them—like in Sunday school when the teacher asks a question.

"Passover started back in Moses's day in the Old Testament. God told Moses to tell Pharaoh to let his people go, and He brought all the plagues on Egypt, and Pharaoh still wouldn't budge. You remember that, right?"

There were some nods of agreement.

"Well, the last plague was that all the firstborn males would die if Pharaoh still refused. So God told Moses to tell the Jewish people to paint their doorposts with lamb's blood to keep the angel of death away. You know the rest of the story. The Jewish babies were 'passed over,' and the Egyptian babies died, including Pharaoh's little boy. The next day, he let the Jews go, and Moses was a hero. Well, any of you guys remember that Moses killed someone long before God used him to deliver the Israelites? Yes, he did. Back when Pharaoh was raising Moses as his own son, he killed an Egyptian guard who was mistreating a Jew. Moses ran off and lived in his own prison wilderness for forty years before

God told him to go back and free his people. I wonder what Moses thought about during those forty years. Probably thought his life was over. Probably figured God couldn't and wouldn't have anything else to do with him. But he did. He had big plans for him. And Moses was a murderer." Preacher sat down and let his words soak in like barbeque sauce.

Another day, he asked if they had heard of the apostle Paul.

Nobody said anything.

"Nobody has heard of Paul?" Preacher shook his head and laughed in disbelief. "Saul of Tarsus who became Paul the Apostle? Paul who wrote eight books in the New Testament, including?" He held his hands up.

There was hesitation until Wes blurted out, "Romans." Preacher raised his arms above his head in triumph, and they all laughed.

"Should have known," Wes mumbled.

"If it weren't for Paul, we wouldn't have most of the New Testament and all of these cool verses that I keep quoting that give us *the* message." He pointed toward the sky. "The message is that Jesus died for us—and that every one of us has a chance. But guess what? He didn't start out that way. His name was originally Saul, and he was the Jewish leaders' henchman. He chased down those new followers of Jesus and had them thrown in jail because he thought they were a threat to the Jewish religion. He even had some killed. He held the cloaks of some Jews while they stoned Stephen, one of Jesus's early followers. That's right—another murderer who was used by God to do good things. Chew on that one for a while."

Another day, Preacher said, "You've all heard of David, the shepherd boy, and how he killed Goliath?"

Wes said, "God used a shepherd boy to do big things, right?"

"Yes, but did you know he was also a murderer and an adulterer?" Preacher asked. "David went on to become king of Israel and had one of his best soldiers killed so that he could have his wife, Bathsheba. Messed up pretty bad, didn't he? But he repented, changed his ways, and became the most famous king in Israel's history. He even wrote most of the book of Psalms in the Bible. 'The Lord is my shepherd.' Heard of that? Yeah. 'Though I walk through the valley of the shadow of death, I will fear no evil for thou art with me.' That was him. And more than that, both of Jesus's parents were descended from him. Pretty cool, huh? God could have thrown him to the wolves, but he didn't. He used him for good things because David turned from his mistakes and allowed God to use him for good. How you like them beans?"

These were the kind of stories that could give a hopeless, lost criminal the will to go on. It gave them hope that maybe they hadn't squandered their lives. They had messed up, but with repentance, there could be a new lease on life. It's never over with God. This was Preacher's message and his mission. And none of his stories drove his message home better than Christ's parables of the lost coin and the lost sheep in Luke. Wes—and most of the other Freaks—loved to hear Preacher tell those two stories, and for good reason.

"Suppose a woman has ten silver coins and loses one. Doesn't she light a lamp, sweep the house, and search carefully until she finds it? And when she finds it, she calls her friends and neighbors together and says, 'Rejoice with me; I have found my lost coin.' In the same way, Jesus says, 'There is rejoicing in the presence of the angels of God over one sinner who repents.'"

Preacher also said, "And how 'bout this one Jesus told? 'Suppose one of you has a hundred sheep and loses one of them. Doesn't he leave the ninety-nine in the open country and go after the lost sheep until he finds it? And when he finds it, he joyfully puts it on his shoulders and goes home. Then, he calls his friends and neighbors together, and says, 'Rejoice with me; I have found my lost sheep.' I tell you that in the same way there will be more rejoicing in heaven over one sinner who repents than over ninety-nine righteous persons who do not need to repent.'"

"Guys, I don't know about you, but I have been that lost coin and that lost sheep. He's talking about us and to us. Jesus said he came to heal the sick like us. It ain't over. It ain't over! It's never too late."

Those powerful words found their way into more than one tough heart in that seemingly godforsaken place, including the heart of Wes Strong. Many of those men who had given up on all hope of forgiveness or a second chance could now see the light of Christ. And Wes knew as well as any of them what it was like to be stuck in a well of despair without hope.

Preacher's words were a light in the dark, a lifeline in the well, a second chance. His words were a blessing to those needy souls as the months and years marched slowly on.

CHAPTER 12

SALVATION

"John Henry Smith," Preacher said matter-of-factly one April day as he sat down beside Wes on the bleachers.

"What?" Wes asked.

"John Henry Smith. That's my real name," Preacher replied.

"What brought that on?" said Wes. "I mean I've been here almost three years, and you've never told me that."

Preacher smiled and looked down at the dirt. "It's time you knew. Not everyone does, but you need to hear it."

They both paused a minute and looked around. The other guys in their corner were all talking about sports, which was the most popular topic of conversation when Preacher wasn't talking. Preacher and Wes were in their own little world.

"So you know I'm in for involuntary manslaughter, right?" Preacher said. Without waiting for a reply, he said, "Know who it was?"

Wes shook his head.

"My wife. I was young, cocky. I loved my wine, but it didn't like me. Made me mean. But that didn't stop me from drinking it every chance I got. I had a good job at the mill. When I wasn't working, I was with my guys: hanging out, drinking, and playing the fool. Most days, I could handle it okay. Made me feel good.

Made me funny. Carlotta put up with it the best she could, but some days she got after me real good about drinking less, staying home, and helping with our daughter. That's right; I got a kid. Lizzie is her name. She'd be about fifteen now I guess."

Preacher stared off into space as if trying to go back in time to another place. Trying to see faces he hadn't seen in many years. Wondering what they might look like today.

"Anyway, one Saturday when Lizzie was about two, I had been out as usual with the guys and drinking it up. Carlotta had been on me lately, and things weren't real good between us at that time. I came in late, and she was all over me. Fussing, telling me I needed to straighten up and stay home more. Let me tell you. If there was one thing I didn't like was some woman telling me what to do. I was a man. I worked hard, and my off time was mine to spend how I liked. Yes, sir. Young, stupid punk. I'd like to go back in time and whup his rear. Beat the living daylight out of him. Try to knock some sense in his head. Anyway, we got to yelling at each other pretty good. She got in my face, and I pushed her back."

He looked down, clenched his teeth, and took a deep breath. "Must have pushed her harder than I thought. She fell back and hit the back of her head right on the corner of the counter. She was out. Blood everywhere. I ran and got the neighbors. They called the hospital, but it was too late. She was gone. One stupid wrong decision, and our lives changed forever. Judge threw me in here quicker than you could say, 'Guilty.' Young, drunk black man needs to be off the streets—thirty years. And Lizzie? My wife's family took her; the courts gave her to them. Never saw her again. I send letters and cards, but they all come back."

"Wow," Wes said. "I had no idea."

"Yeah, well. So, they sent me here to pay my dues. I was twenty-eight and felt like my life was over. Angry, man, I was angry. Hated life, hated the judge, hated my wife for getting in my face, hated my wife's family for taking my daughter—I had plenty of blame to go around. No way it was my fault. She made me do it. She slipped and fell. Not my fault. I came in here with enough bad attitude for ten of these guys. And I was ready to take it out on anybody who got in my way. Better not mess with me. I'll kick your tail. Back then, there wasn't the gangs and the drugs. There was just angry men who needed to vent. And I vented. I was in fights all the time. I probably hold the record for time in solitary in the first two years in here."

He looked down as if struggling with the weight of the painful words. Things he didn't like to think about anymore, much less talk about. Thoughts he had buried a long time ago. But it was a story Wes needed to hear. There would be a point. Finally, he went on.

"There was one old black man in here they called the Rev. He sat right here on these very seats. He would preach the gospel to anyone within earshot. Including me. But let me tell you, I wasn't having any of it. I gave that man a terrible time. I didn't need no old man telling me what to do. To repent and change my ways. So angry and cocky. I didn't need his religion to straighten me out. Just stay out of my way, old man. But he wouldn't give up on me. Always trying to sit me down and talk some sense in me. It went on for those first two years. If I wasn't in solitary and was allowed in the rec yard, then he was trying to talk to me. It got to the point that before he could start, I would start making fun of him just to keep him quiet. I was merciless. Taunting him and laughing at him. Making jokes about him. But he just smiled and took it. Never got upset.

"Well, there was one guy I had several fights with. Red was his name. We were both trying to be top dog in the pen. One day in the yard, I was in the Rev's face giving him a hard time when Red came up behind me with a shiver in his hand to do me in. The

Rev saw him just in time and pushed me out of the way." Preacher slowly shook his head as if the words were too painful to speak.

Wes looked down. He had no idea any of this had happened and didn't know what to say.

After a minute, Preacher gathered himself and went on. "Wes, that man took a knife for me. That good man who had no reason to help me pushed me out of the way and took what was mine. Rev's life would actually have been better if Red had killed me instead of him after the way I treated him. I can still see him taking his last breaths right here. And you know what his last words were?"

Wes looked up.

"Jesus loves you," Preacher shook his head, still in disbelief. "The man is dying, and he's still worried about me. Me—who had never said a kind word to him in my life." Preacher wiped away a tear from each eye and slowly shook his head. "That man saved both my lives that day—my earthly one and my eternal one. After that, I didn't have much to say for a long time. I took a long, hard look at the way I had lived and realized the problem wasn't everyone else. It was me. That's what happens when you reach rock bottom. You stop looking out and start looking in. And Jesus will always be there waiting. He was for me, and he was for you. Wes, when you were in solitary the night before you came out and you prayed for help, was that prayer answered?"

"How did you know that?" Wes said.

"Lucky guess," Preacher replied. "Was that prayer answered?"

"Yes," Wes said, looking deep into Preacher's eyes.

"Wes, what is the first verse of Romans chapter 8?"

"There is now no condemnation for those who are in Christ Jesus."

"That's right. No condemnation for those who believe in Jesus. We are forgiven. And there is no limit to that forgiveness for those who believe in Him. It never ends. Now, what about Romans 8:28?"

"All things work together for good for those who love God."

"Very good," Preacher said. "Not some things—all things. He can take everything and work it good if we love Him. And then in verse 32, it says that He did not withhold his own Son but gave Him up for all of us. Will He not give us everything else? He sent His own Son to die for our sins, so that we might have eternal life. Can you imagine? His own Son. Now what about the last verse in that chapter?"

"I am absolutely sure that not even death or life, nor angels or demons, nor things present or future, nor things high or low, principalities or kingdoms, darkness or light will ever separate us from the love of Christ."

"Wow, you have been studying. Okay, so there is absolutely nothing we can do to separate us from His love. Not a thing. By His grace alone, God forgives us. We can't earn it. He sent His Son to die for our sins so that we might have eternal life, and He has good plans for us. Sound familiar?"

"Sounds like my grandmother," Wes said.

"That's right," Preacher said. "Sounds like Grandma. See why I like Romans chapter 8? All right, Wes, here's the point. This wasn't written for just the rich folks in their fancy houses or all the do-gooders out there. It was written for all of us sinners here on God's green earth: me and you and everybody out there. And by the way, Paul was in a Roman prison when he wrote those words.

"Wes, I don't know why all this stuff happened. Or why any bad things happen to anybody. I don't know why I never met my father. I don't know why your father treated you like he did. But I do know it was not your fault. And I know that there is a God up there that created everything, and if He's smart enough to create all this, then He's smart enough to take care of me. He's God, and I'm not. He's in control, and I am not. Do you understand what I'm saying?"

Without waiting for an answer, Preacher said, "It was not your fault, Wes. You didn't do anything to deserve your childhood. Neither did I. It was not your fault. Do you hear me?"

Wes had been looking straight into Preacher's eyes, and hearing those words for the third time broke the emotional dam that Wes had been laboring on for many years—brick by brick. He hung his head and began to cry softly. He didn't care who saw or where he was. Suddenly, it felt like the weight of the world had been lifted off of his shoulders.

Preacher put his hand on Wes's shoulder and continued, "Wes, let it go. Let the past go. It's gone. It doesn't have to control your future any longer. You can only control the here and now. Let Christ in—and let Him take over. From here on out, live for Him. He will guide you."

Wes sobbed quietly for a minute. Everything else went on as usual in the rec yard—except that a man's soul was being saved. In the middle of a dusty, dingy prison yard in Podunk, South Carolina. And just like in the Parable of the Lost Coin, the angels rejoiced in the presence of God.

Finally, Wes said, "I surrender, Preacher. I don't want to be the person I've been. I want to live for Jesus."

Preacher smiled a huge smile and said, "That's the best news ever, Wes. Say this prayer with me. 'Father, I know I have sinned. I am asking for your forgiveness. I know that you sent your son to die for my sins. I surrender my life to you.'"

Wes repeated the prayer. Afterward, they both looked up through their tears and laughed heartily.

CHAPTER 13

TIME TRIALS

The next day, Preacher was sitting at his usual spot in the corner. He smiled and stood up when he saw Wes coming. He held up his hand to high-five Wes.

"My man. My new man," Preacher said with a laugh and a pat on Wes's back. "Have a seat."

"What now? What happens now?" Wes felt like he had signed up for one of those five-step recovery plans.

"Well, it won't be easy. We aren't magically transformed overnight into perfect angels. Wish we were. We still have to deal with what this world throws at us, its values, and our old sinful nature. Being saved definitely is not a license to go out and sin all we want to just because we are saved. Jesus told the prostitute that He saved from being stoned by the Pharisees to 'go and sin no more.' He's talking to us too. God doesn't promise us an easy path. But he does promise to be with us every step of the way. In Philippians, Paul says, 'He who began a good work in you will perfect it until the day of Jesus Christ.' Sanctification is a big word that means day by day, little by little, God is transforming us into the likeness of His Son. You will win some and lose some, but God will never give up on us. Lots of days, you will feel like you are not growing or like you are stuck in a rut, but God is always working behind the scenes to transform us. We can't see the big picture, but He can. We just have to ask for His help in making decisions and trust in His plan for us. When we realize we've made a mistake, and you will still make mistakes, we ask for forgiveness and move on. Don't dwell on it or wallow in it, and definitely don't beat yourself up. Keep looking forward and trying to do the best you can. What do you think?"

"I'll give it my best shot," Wes replied.

"That's all you can do. It's all any us can do. Now you understand that there is nothing we do to earn His grace. It's a free gift. Our obedience is a result of this grace, not obedience in order to earn grace. That's a tough one for us humans. One of the hardest things is to just let go and let God take control. Trust is a simple word, but it's so tough to do. I try to look at it like a bank—a faith bank. Every day, we have to make a choice to either worry and strive on our own to work things out or make a decision to trust that God is in control and will work it all out for our good. Trust and worry are not compatible. We have to make a deposit in our faith bank. When you make that deposit and trust Him in the little things, then when the harder things come along, it gets easier to trust Him. You can fall back on the capital you have built up in that bank. Get it?" Preacher asked.

Wes nodded.

After a few minutes of silence, Wes smiled and asked, "By the way, should I call you John, John Henry, or Mr. Smith?"

"Preacher is just fine. And you just keep that information to yourself, okay?"

Wes laughed and said, "No problem."

Over the next several months, Wes dove into the devotionals and religious books Preacher shared with him. He was a ready student, eager to soak up all he could. A whole new world had been opened up to him. It was like he had been at the door but just never went in. Things were becoming so much clearer.

One day, Preacher grabbed Wes by the arm and took him off to the side for a little private conference. "I've got something serious I want to talk to you about, Wes."

"Uh-oh," Wes answered.

"No, no. Not bad," Preacher responded. "I know you were a big runner. You've told me some things, and I've read some things. You had some potential, I think, before you took this little detour. I'm guessing that potential is still there. You won't be in here forever—at most, you've got maybe two more years or so—and I think maybe I have finally convinced you that your life isn't over. Why don't you start running again? What do you think?"

Wes looked down for a long minute. "Oh, I don't know. That dream died when I came through those gates over there. For a long time, when I was first arrested, I wanted to run in a bad way. A very bad way. Not necessarily to escape but to punish myself for what I had done. Self-loathing is a big running motivator. Besides, where would I run? There is not much room in here, and I don't see a track. Unless you can get the warden to build us one."

"No, I don't think that's happening, but there is another choice. You see the outer perimeter electric fence with the guard towers at the corners, and then there is about ten feet before you get to the inner fence that we can touch over there? That's ten feet of dirt that surrounds this place. Goes from one side of the big entry gate clear around to the other side without any interruptions. How far do you think that is?"

Wes was looking at the area of no-man's land that Preacher was pointing out. He thought hard for a second and then replied, "Close to half a mile, I guess."

"Yeah, that's kinda what I thought too," Preacher replied. "What if I could get the warden to let you run in there while we are in the rec yard?"

"What? How in the world are you going to pull that off?" Wes asked.

"You just leave that up to me, my boy," Preacher said with a wink. "Mr. Warden owes me a favor or two for certain information I have been able to supply him from time to time. And that is between me and you, you understand?"

"Got it," Wes said as he stood up. He looked around at the no-man's land again for a long minute and then looked at Preacher with a slight nod. "Okay, then. Guess it wouldn't hurt to ask."

Several weeks later, the Freaks all stood on their bleachers and watched as the guards escorted Wes through several locked gates and into the no-man's land. Wes looked around at his new territory and then over to his friends. With a nod to them, he slowly started to jog from one gate to the other. He went very slowly and deliberately back and forth for about twenty minutes. They might as well as given him the key to the front gate. Wes suddenly felt free again. Then, he stopped and walked for a few minutes before he told the guards he was finished for the day.

They escorted him back through the gates and into the rec yard. Big Frank was waiting to escort him over to their corner.

"How was it?" Big Frank asked.

Wes nodded as he headed straight to Preacher and shook his hand. With tears in his eyes, he said, "Thank you."

The next several weeks were some of the happiest Wes spent behind bars—if such a thing could be possible. He felt like he had a new lease on life. As a new Christian, he felt like a sponge. He couldn't soak up enough of the Bible. There was so much to learn, and he felt so far behind. Fortunately, Preacher was a ready source of information. He supplied books and tapes. And, of course, Preacher didn't mind talking religion anytime. Wes was especially drawn to the writings of Paul—his sufferings, his letters to the early churches on behavior, and how to be content no matter the circumstances. It was all so new to Wes, but he felt like the eyes of his mind had suddenly been opened. Everything made so much more sense.

"The Holy Spirit," Preacher said to him one day.

"What?" Wes replied.

"Once you are a believer, the Holy Spirit is freed to take up residence within us to help us understand. He's been there all along, but until you are ready to receive Christ, He cannot do his work in you. You've let him loose. That's why it suddenly seems clearer. Pretty amazing, huh?"

Of course, along with this was his newfound freedom to run. For the first time, Wes felt completely unburdened. He felt like he wasn't running from anything or trying to punish himself for his mistakes. He just ran. He thanked God for this opportunity, for the beauty of the day, and for loving him. This also seemed like a new experience. He could run easy or harder if he wanted to without an agenda. He could use this time to pray as he ran—to talk to God, to meditate on the things he had read or discussed with Preacher. When his body got in the rhythm of running, his mind was free to wander to new experiences with God—and new levels of understanding and clarity. It was almost like he had to defeat the body, to bring it under control, before the mind was truly free. And once the ears of his soul were open, he could hear what God was softly saying. Some days a one-hour run felt like ten minutes as he entered this zone. All he could do on days like that was smile, shake his head, and say "Wow!"

Wes ran every day at first. He had so much to think about, and the runs really helped him process everything that was happening and the things he was learning in his studies. He usually used the first sixty minutes of rec time to run and the last thirty minutes to talk or listen to Preacher.

After about two months of his new routine, Preacher said, "Wes, I've been watching you run. I want to know what you are doing out there when you run."

Wes frowned. Did he look funny when he was in the zone—or maybe his stride looked funny? "What do you mean?"

Preacher waved his hand and pointed to the other guys. "Well, me and the guys have been watching you, and some days, you run back and forth, back and forth, and you look just the same. You never speed up or slow down. Then, some days, you run really fast in one direction and then slow in the other direction. And then some days, you just fly the whole time like the Boyz over there are after you. What's up with all that?"

Wes smiled. "Oh, I didn't know what you were talking about. I thought I was running weird or something. I just kind of figured I ought to make my time count out there and do some training like I used to in the old days. When you run distance, you have to build a base to get you in shape to cover a long distance, and you do that by running long, fairly slow runs. But if you want to get faster at it, you have to run some sprints faster than the pace you would run in a race to get your body use to running at a faster pace for a longer distance. Then, once in a while you have to go all out to see what you can do. A time trial they call it. You're getting your body stronger for what lies ahead—for when it counts."

"Wait. Explain that last part again," Preacher interrupted. "The part about the time trial."

After Wes repeated his explanation, Preacher started laughing loudly. He slapped Big Frank on the back and said, "Time trial, huh? What did you say—getting stronger for what lies ahead?"

Wes smiled and nodded.

Preacher said, "Fellows, that's it! That's exactly what we are doing in here. Time trials. Getting stronger for what lies ahead. The Good Lord is training all of us to get stronger for Him for what lies ahead. Building our faith. Time trials. Now we know."

They all laughed together at the new revelation. Down the road, Wes would think back on that conversation many, many times as another example of Romans 8:28—and how God can use things in our lives for our good and His ultimate glory.

Good can come out of bad. Preacher had summed up the prison experience perfectly in a way they all could understand.

CHAPTER 14

REVENGE

O ver the next six months, Wes felt his running legs coming back. It had been a long layoff, and he had gained a few pounds in addition to the atrophy in his leg muscles. It was only natural that it would take a while to get back in shape. He continued to work on his own training program, which included a lot of easy miles, some intervals, and some time trials. It was just like the old days—except he didn't have a race on the horizon. He put that thought out of his mind and enjoyed his new level of freedom. Freedom for his mind to go anywhere while he was running. The walls, fences, and guards would all disappear once his legs started moving. Maybe it was the lactic acid building up in his leg muscles, but it felt as though once the body was in a steady state of flow—as if it had been brought into submission— the mind was free to go anywhere.

And travel he did. Wes began to allow himself to think about the future. He tried to leave the past just where it was: in the past. Like Preacher said, you can only control the moment you are in. He focused on that, but he couldn't help but wonder about what lay in store in his future. What kind of work would he be able to find once he was released? Wes had continued his online courses for a general degree in psychology and was making significant progress. Now that he had turned his life over to Christ, he began to think of ways he could serve God once he got out. Wes understood that his salvation was safe. There was nothing he could do to earn it or improve on it. His motivations were pure. He just wanted to bring glory to God. Good works in response to his salvation, not good works to earn it. Christ had already done that work for him.

Wes began to think about ways he could help other youth not make the mistakes he had made. He knew there were a lot of kids out there with worse family situations than his; maybe he could help them. There were so many families without fathers in the picture. Surely there would be something he could do. If nothing else, maybe he could volunteer somewhere. He wasn't sure how that would work with his record and everything, but he shared those thoughts with Preacher.

"Sounds like the Spirit is getting hold of you, my boy. That's a good thing. Like I've always said, I'm sure God has big plans for you. Sound familiar?"

"Oh yeah, I had almost forgotten about Grandmom," Wes said. "Maybe she can get something going for me with her connections in heaven."

Preacher laughed and said, "Well, in the meantime, I'll pass it on to the warden here. We'll see if he can do anything."

"Thanks, Preacher. Thanks for everything," Wes said.

"Look, Wes, there is something else you need to be thinking about."

Wes looked at him curiously.

Preacher said, "Forgiveness."

"What?"

"Forgiveness. We've talked about letting the past go and moving on, right?"

Wes nodded.

"Well, part of that letting go is forgiving those who have harmed us. I know it's a tough one, but as Christians, we are called to it by Christ himself. 'Forgive those who harm you, and by the same measure you will be forgiven,' He told us. Wes, I don't know if you will ever see your father again, but if you want to cut the last link in that ball and chain you've been dragging around for so long, you need to forgive him."

"I know." Wes looked off into the distance. "I've been reading those words too and chewing on them as you would say. It's a tough chew and hard to swallow, but I'm working on it."

"Okay, then," Preacher said. "You keep working on it because there's another one too."

"There is?"

Preacher pursed his lips and poked Wes's chest. "You, my man."

"Me?"

"You made a mistake, and you ended up in here. Somebody lost his life. There is a family out there still hurting, and you had something to do with it. You've repented of your sins and started a new relationship with Christ. God forgives you, and that family may or may not, but you might think about reaching out to them. Tell them how sorry you are for their loss and how you hope to help other young folks from making the same mistakes you made. You might not hear from them, but at least by doing that, you can let the old Wes heal and cut that chain too. The circle will be complete. You forgive those who have hurt you, and you ask for forgiveness from those you've hurt."

"Hadn't thought about that," Wes replied slowly. "Guess I need to work on that one too."

"Yeah, you do that," Preacher replied. "Okay, that's enough to think about for today. Let's go get some grub. I think it's about that time."

Life behind bars is all about routine. A routine a prisoner has very little control over. Everything is by the schedule. You can almost predict where an inmate will be every second of every day. That's just the way it has to be. Sometimes that can work against you if someone wants to do you harm. Preacher still made sure Wes had his bodyguards whenever he was out of his cell. Wes wasn't the only one who had his own escorts, but he was definitely Preacher's favorite. He had come a long way since he first got there, and Preacher truly felt like God had big things in store for him. It was just a hunch, but he wanted to make sure nothing got in the way of those plans.

Devious still held a grudge against Wes, and seeing him enjoy his extra running freedom was the last straw. He didn't like seeing someone else getting extra privileges that he wasn't getting, especially his rivals. Things seemed a little too good on the other side of the rec yard to Devious. "I think it's about time to shake things up over there," he said. "I've had about enough of Preacher man and his boy."

He was still determined to get his revenge. Grudges are not forgotten inside prison walls. With nothing but time on his hands, Devious could afford to wait. The war of words between the two groups had never ceased, but in the last few months, it accelerated. The pushing and shoving when the inmates entered and left the rec yard had also picked up. Devious decided he would use that to his advantage.

Wes continued to run through the winter, when the weather permitted, which was most days that year. The days were getting warmer, which meant the inmates did not need their prison-issue jackets in the rec yard every day. It was not unusual that some of them wore them in the yard while others did not. Devious used this cover to smuggle a shank into the rec yard one day. His shank was a six-inch piece of metal that had been filed down into a very sharp knife. It had tape wrapped around one end for a handle. Used in the right way by the right person, it would be deadly.

Devious just needed the chance to get close enough as they exited the yard to bury his weapon into Wes's back. He figured killing Wes would kill two birds with one stone, so to speak, since he was Preacher's favorite. Devious would do the deed in the middle of the crowd to show everyone he was the boss. He knew there would be little chance of the guards seeing him. It would be done quickly as they exited when everyone was together at the gate.

Devious had his guys watching to see when he had maneuvered into position. When he nodded, they were to start pushing at the front of the crowd to create a distraction. Devious had been trying for several days to get close enough with no success. He would need to slip behind them without his entourage to not attract attention.

On Friday, he made sure he was within striking distance.

Wes was exiting with Preacher. Big Frank was on the right of Preacher, which left Wes's left side exposed. With a nod to his boys, Devious seized his opportunity. He would strike quickly and disappear into the crowd. He would have his revenge.

After Devious gave the signal, the pushing started at the front. As everyone looked forward to see what was going on, Devious pulled out his weapon and quickly prepared to slip it between Wes's back ribs. It was not his first time using a knife, and he knew exactly where to place his dagger to reach Wes's liver and celiac artery, so he would bleed out in a matter of minutes.

As Devious pulled back to make his thrust, Preacher glanced at Wes. A small glimmer of light reflecting off of the weapon caught Preacher's eye. In a split second, he pushed Wes to the side and lunged to stop Devious. Devious had already started his forward motion and buried his shank in Preacher's abdomen with all his might.

Wes fell to the ground as Preacher fell on top of him. Big Frank let out a yell and sprung on Devious in a flash. With his massive hands, he grabbed Devious on both sides of his head, and with a quick twist, he broke Devious's neck, killing him instantly.

Wes got to his knees, pulled off his shirt, and applied pressure to Preacher's wound. "Help, get help," he screamed at the top of his lungs as everyone quickly gathered around. Preacher was bleeding profusely and blinking hard as if to comprehend what was happening. They both knew it was bad.

"Wes," Preacher said softly as he reached for Wes's hands. "There's not time. It's okay. It's okay. Listen to me—remember what you've learned and be strong. God loves you. I'm so proud of you. Run for me. Run for me." His last words tumbled out slowly as he slipped away.

"No, no," Wes screamed. He felt for a pulse and realized Preacher was gone. This man who had saved Wes's eternal soul had now saved his earthly life also. Wes rested his head on Preacher's chest and sobbed loudly.

Big Frank let out a scream and put his hand on Wes's shoulder. "I'm sorry. I'm sorry," he kept repeating. "I should have been watching better."

The guards rushed in to restore order before an all-out riot broke loose. With the abrupt deaths of both of the rival faction's leaders, the two sides stopped in stunned silence. The guards hustled the inmates out of the rec yard, but Preacher's friend's gathered in a silent circle around the body.

The guards carried Devious's body out of the yard. All was quiet in the yard except for the soft crying and sniffling of the men who looked on Preacher as much more than a friend or fellow inmate. He was the one who made sense out of that place, who held things together, who pointed them to a life beyond those walls. What would happen now?

Even the guards were stunned by the quick turn of events. They had a lot of respect for Preacher and the way he had turned his life around behind bars. He had such a positive impact on so many inmates. He was the soothing balm in a raw, tense environment. He was the lid on the pressure cooker of prison life. Would anybody be able to take his place? Out of this deep sense of respect, they allowed Preacher's friends to stay with his body until the coroner arrived. When it was finally time to remove the body, the guards told the guys they had five more minutes.

Wes raised his head off of Preacher's chest and slowly unclasped the cross that Preacher always wore around his neck. He took a long look at the cross, bowed his head, and slowly raised it above his head in his fist.

Slowly, all the other Freaks raised their fists in a show of silent respect for their fallen leader.

CHAPTER 15

LEGACY

The prison was placed on lockdown for a week after the murder. Meals were delivered to the inmates' cells, and showers were every other day—and only in strictly supervised groups. The warden knew how quickly these things could get out of hand, and he wasn't taking any chances.

With the leaders of both sides gone, the sense of hierarchy and order was gone. Chaos could happen any second over the smallest incident if the two sides were allowed contact. The warden was hoping a cool-down period would help ease the tension.

He also thought it would be a good idea to talk to some of the inmates individually to see if he could get a feel for how things were going to be and see if he could convince them to help keep the peace. Wes was one of the first inmates he chose to talk with.

Several guards escorted Wes to the meeting room.

In the days following the death of Preacher, Wes had clutched Preacher's necklace and struggled to make sense of it all. He kept replaying the whole terrible episode in his head, wondering if he could have done anything to prevent it. Wes found it ironic that Preacher died the same way the Reverend had. He also thought it was ironic that this poor black inmate who had been a father figure to him had told him that he was proud of him when he had never heard those words from his own father.

Wes struggled to stay out of that dark well he knew so well. Wes kept hearing Preacher's last words in his head, but he didn't know if he could be strong and have faith. Not after all he had been through. *God, why? If things happen for a reason, and you have good plans for all of us, then why this? Why now?*

The warden said, "Wes, I know you and Preacher were very close. We all had a lot of respect for him and the way he turned his life around. He was a good man, and I'm sorry. But life is going to go on, and we have to decide how it's going to be. That's where I'd like to ask for your help. Don't let his death be in vain. We need some calm heads in here that will not let this place deteriorate into some type of bloodbath of revenge killings. Can I count on you to talk to your guys?"

Wes sat hunched over, but he glanced at the warden. After a long second, he nodded and said, "I'll try."

"Don't forget the lessons Preacher was trying to teach. Let that be his legacy, okay?"

"Yes, sir," Wes replied. "Can I ask one favor in return, sir?"

"What's that, Wes?"

"Is there any way you could get me the address of someone in Preacher's family, preferably his daughter? I'd like to send them a letter to tell them about the man he became in here. I'd like them to know how many lives he changed."

"Sure, son," the warden replied.

That night, Wes had a dream where he was a witness to another murder in the rec yard. He saw a younger, much different Preacher. He saw the Rev taking the knife for Preacher. He heard the Rev say, "Jesus loves you." He saw Preacher staring incredulously at the dead man in total disbelief that he had saved his life. Finally, he saw Preacher kneeling in his cell and surrendering to Christ.

When Wes woke up, he stared into the darkness for a second before he rolled out of his bed and onto his knees. Resting his head on top of his clasped hands, he prayed, "Dear God in heaven, I don't know why this happened, but I'm going to trust that you have a good plan for all of us like Preacher said. His life will not be in vain. I will do all I can to carry on his message, your message. Please take good care of him in heaven. Amen."

The next day, there was an announcement that the inmates would be allowed back in the rec yard in two separate groups for forty-five minutes each. The warden felt like this would give the two groups time to talk. He hoped the leaders could calm the frayed emotions.

When the Freaks went out, all twenty-three guys gathered quietly on the bench where Preacher had always held court. Wes was one of the last to arrive after he and Big Frank had a word as they entered the yard. Big Frank had not been arrested for killing Devious since no one could say for sure what happened to Devious. Big Frank was still there to escort Wes to the rec yard.

Wes immediately took charge as he walked up and faced the solemn group. "Guys, we all loved Preacher. His death will not be in vain, but there will be no revenge. Justice has been served, and Devious is gone. The best thing we can do to honor Preacher is to carry his message on and to live lives that would make him proud. Agreed?" He glanced at Big Frank.

Big Frank crossed his huge arms and gave his most intimidating stare at the group.

"Agreed?" Wes repeated.

Everyone nodded.

"Good," Wes said. "Do you remember the story Preacher told about Joseph and how his brothers sold him into slavery? And when they were reunited years later, Joseph told them how they meant evil in what they did, but God meant it for good. That now he could save the Jewish people during the drought. Well Devious meant this for evil, but Preacher would want us to believe that God means it for good. Good will somehow come out of this."

Wes then launched into his first "sermon" to the group, going on for the next fifteen minutes without stopping. Preacher would have been proud. Just as Preacher had taken over after the Rev had saved his life, Wes knew it was his responsibility to step into the huge shoes left by Preacher. He didn't feel qualified, but he was counting on God to lead him. Like Preacher had said, "God doesn't call the qualified; he qualifies the called!"

The period after Preacher's death went much better than the warden expected. There were some words exchanged, but there was no violence. Security was stepped up, and more guards patrolled the rec yard for the next several months.

Wes became the new leader of the Freaks. No one emerged as the leader of the Boyz, and they seemed lost without Devious. For the time being, they seemed more interested in maintaining their flow of drugs and contraband from the outside. There were some serious habits that had to be supported. The guards turned a blind eye to some of this trafficking for the time being, hoping it would help take the edge off and help maintain control.

Wes was eventually able to start running again—but not as much as he had been before. He felt a new responsibility to be in the yard to talk to the guys. Since his salvation, he had been like a sponge soaking up all the biblical knowledge he could. It was being put to good use along with the stories that Preacher told. He lacked Preacher's charisma, but the more he talked, the better he became at relaying a message of hope to his rapt audience. It also helped to throw in some "remember when" stories about things Preacher had said and done to lighten things up.

Wes let it be known that any and all would be welcome to hear what he had to say. Watts and a few others began to hang out with the Freaks, touched by Preacher's sacrifice and his legacy. They wanted to see for themselves what he was about. What led him to sacrifice himself for someone else? It was a foreign concept to them. It was Wes's turn to do the talking, and Watts's turn to listen. Wes enjoyed turning the tables on Watts and having a little fun with him.

"Watts, you ever heard of Saul? How 'bout Paul?"

"Naw, man," Watts replied. "He didn't hang out in my 'hood."

Wes would laugh and launch into the story of how Saul became Paul and all the good he did with his life after he surrendered to Christ. Each time, he shared a new story of redemption for Watts, he would be sure to talk about God's gift of His Son for our sins. How He died for us. Trying to mimic the things he had seen Preacher do over and over to try to reach the guys.

Slowly, he could tell he was getting Watts's attention. He seemed to be listening a little closer and hanging around with the Freaks more often.

One day, during the morning dishwashing ritual, Watts said, "Hey, man, you got an extra Bible layin' around anywhere? I want to read a little about that Paul dude."

"Sure, Watts. I can set you up," Wes replied. "I tell you what. I'll even show you where to start. The book of Romans. You start looking at it, and we'll talk about it while we wash dishes. Deal?"

"Sounds cool, man," Watts replied.

Wes had to smile as he recalled his early conversations with Preacher. *Looks like things have come full circle.* Preacher's memory was alive and well among the friends he left behind—but in none more so than in Wes Strong.

CHAPTER 16

SECOND CHANCE

Almost a year had gone by since Preacher's death. Wes was the accepted leader of the Jesus Freaks. He had found a new mission in life with his Bible study, preaching to the Freaks, and running. Things had settled down in the prison. It was almost as if the death of Devious had removed a lot of the tension in the air. The newer inmates did not seem to have the gang loyalty or need for violence that had been pervasive during Devious's reign. The new guys were mostly in for meth manufacturing or stealing. As long as they could get a little fix now and then, they didn't bother anybody and served their time peacefully for the most part.

Wes and the Freaks still did the best they could to reach those they could with the message of Jesus Christ. Wes had been behind bars for almost five years. He would have liked to say it had flown by, but it hadn't. There had been a lot of dark days, but thanks to Preacher, he had come through it a better person. He had been saved, and he had gotten enough college credits to be classified as a senior.

Wes knew Romans 8:28 was true. He felt God's love and gentle but firm hand on his life every day. He was facing just one more year behind bars, which gave him something to look forward to. *One more year*, he thought while he ran. It was scary to consider how he would be accepted on the outside, but he had decided to trust in God and His good provision. *It will all work out.*

As he finished one of his normal shifts in the cafeteria, a guard came to tell him the warden wanted to see him. He glanced at Watts with wide eyes as Wes wondered what this could be about. Wes put down his towel, took off his apron, and patted Watts on the back as he followed the guard.

Thoughts raced through Wes's head as they walked down the hall. It had to be pretty important for the warden to summon him since he had talked to him only a few times during his stay. He knew Preacher had become a pretty close confidant of the warden as his stature had continued to grow among the Freaks, but these had been calmer days with little need for contact with upper management. Wes sure didn't have any big news from the "inside" to share with the warden.

In the small meeting room where Wes had met the warden after Preacher's death, the warden waited with a woman who looked like a school principal. With her blond hair pulled up and her business dress, she reminded him of his mom when she was dressed up for church.

"Come in, Wes, and have a seat," the warden said. "This is Joan Bridges. She is the director of the Bowers-Rodgers Shelter in Greenwood. Are you familiar with it?"

Wes glanced back and forth from the warden to this mysterious lady and slowly shook his head no. *What in the world could this be about?* His curiosity was piqued, but he relaxed a little as he realized he must not be in trouble.

"Hi, Wes," she said. "The Bowers-Rodgers Home is a shelter for abused and neglected children that houses up to fifteen kids, mostly under the age of thirteen. If parents are arrested or can't properly take care of their children, the Department of Social

Services steps in and brings the children to our shelter until the courts decide what to do. Sometimes, they eventually go back to their parents or other family members, and sometimes they are assigned to foster parents. They are usually with us for no more than ninety days."

Wes nodded, but he was wondering what in the world it had to do with him. He didn't have any close relatives, so he knew he couldn't have anybody there. And he had never even had sex, so he knew he didn't have any unknown kids out there. Maybe they were looking for prisoners to talk to the kids.

The warden said, "Wes, the state of South Carolina is starting a new early-release program for inmates who have shown significant change while incarcerated. Part of the requirement is that they have to be released to the supervision of an agency that can provide at least part-time employment and oversight. It's kind of like having a parole officer with you every day to make sure you are doing okay. If you slip up, you are immediately brought back to prison to serve the remainder of your sentence. Wes, Preacher had been singing your praises for a number of months before he died, and he told me that if anybody ever deserved to get out early, it was you. I don't normally put a lot of stock in prisoner's opinions, but Preacher was a pretty good judge of character in his later years. He also said you had expressed an interest in helping other kids avoid the mistakes you made? Correct? Are you getting where this is heading, son?"

Wes lowered his head, raised the neck of his prison-issue shirt up to his eyes, and began to cry softly. "Yes, sir. I think so. I'm sorry."

The warden smiled and looked at Ms. Bridges. "I don't get to give out good news to inmates very often, so today is a good day. Ms. Bridges has agreed to provide you a part-time job as a youth counselor at Bowers-Rodgers. You will report to her and to your parole officer. You will always have to be with another counselor when you are with the kids for everyone's protection. We think you have something to offer the kids, and we'd like to give you a second chance. What do you think?"

Wes looked up through his tears and nodded, "Yes sir, of course. Wow, I can't believe it."

"Good," the warden said. "We thought you might say that." He smiled at Ms. Bridges.

As the gravity of this unexpected gift settled in, a sudden thought hit Wes. "What about the guys, sir?"

"What do you mean, son?" the warden asked.

"We're a pretty tight group with our Bible study and everything. Since Preacher died, I, um, well I have tried to ..."

"Lead them?" the warden said. "We've noticed."

"Is there any way I could come back once a week or every other week to lead a Bible study with them?"

"I think that could be arranged," the warden replied. "We realize how they look up to you, and having them see you do well on the outside will give them hope. So, yes, we can work that out."

Wes looked at Ms. Bridges and said, "Can I ask you a question? Why me?"

She smiled and said, "This is a win-win for everybody, Wes. You get a second chance to start your life over, and like I said earlier, we think you can have a significant impact on our kids. They desperately need a good male role model, but they also need to see that it's never too late to start over if you make a mistake."

"Are you a Christian organization?" Wes asked.

"Absolutely, we were founded by a local Baptist church that has an excellent minister. Anthony Hogan has a doctorate in New Testament studies and leads a wonderful Bible study on Sunday nights. I'm sure he would love to have you."

"Any other questions?" the warden asked.

With a huge grin on his face, Wes said, "I guess just one. When?"

"Oh yeah. Kind of important," the warden said with a laugh. "Actually, tomorrow."

"Tomorrow?" Wes replied. "Wow."

"One of our board members has a small rental house near our home and has agreed to let you stay there rent-free for six months. When you earn a little money, they'll probably ask for a small rent," Ms. Bridges added.

"Wow. This just gets better and better," Wes said. "I hope I can live up to everyone's expectations. Thank you so much. Can I break it to the guys myself this afternoon?"

"Sure. I thought you might want to." The warden extended his hand for a handshake.

"See you tomorrow, Wes," Ms. Bridges said.

"Ma'am, may I hug you?" Wes asked shyly.

"Absolutely," she said with a laugh.

"Thank you. Thank you so much," Wes said as he softly gave his new guardian angel a hug.

That afternoon, Wes didn't have on his running clothes as he entered the recreation yard with Big Frank. "I need to talk to all the guys, Frank."

"Okay, sounds serious," Frank replied.

After all the Jesus Freaks gathered around their bench, Wes stood up to address them. His chin started quivering, and he stopped and started several times.

Big Frank said, "Spit it out, boy. They transferring you or something?"

"Better," Wes finally said. "I'm getting out tomorrow. Early release."

"What?" the guys said in unison.

"I'm sorry," Wes said softly.

"Sorry. Don't you be sorry, boy," Big Frank said.

They all jumped up to congratulate Wes on his good fortune. All the guys gathered around Wes and patted him on his back.

"Man, that is wonderful! We will miss you though."

After a few minutes of celebration, Wes explained the details to his friends. "I did get the warden to agree to let me come back once a week or so to do a Bible study, so we will still see each other."

Watts said, "Wait a minute. How do you get out first, man? I'm a lot prettier than you! I tell you what though: I may take over your preaching spot."

"I'll hold you to that," Wes said happily.

It was a reason to celebrate when one of their friends was released. They were all happy about his good fortune. It was like a small part of them was getting out too.

Early release was even better. It gave all the guys reason to hope.

CHAPTER 17

A NEW LIFE

N eedless to say, Wes slept very little that night. He alternated spending time on his knees thanking God for this second chance and thinking about his new life. It happened so quickly that he could hardly believe it. He was scared of going to sleep because he was afraid it might all be a dream. It was too good to be true, and there was no time to prepare. How in the world would he know how to help these needy kids?

Dear God, thank you so much. I am trusting you to lead me and show me the way. Please let me have a positive impact on these kids' lives. My faith is in you.

The next morning, Big Frank was there as always to escort him to the cafeteria. Frank was smiling so big it looked like he was the one who was leaving. When the door to Wes's cell opened, Frank gave him a bear hug, lifted him off the ground, and laughed.

Wes worked a short shift in the cafeteria—basically long enough to say good-bye to his coworkers. When he entered the eating area with his food tray, the other Jesus Freaks stood up and gave him a standing ovation. It was tough for Wes. Those guys were like family to him—the only family he had known for five years. They had been through so much together: life and death struggles every day in this world and the next. Who would have ever thought Wes would find God and himself in this place? And now it was time to leave and to say good-bye to his friends. He did his best to keep it light through breakfast, just cutting up with the guys as usual. He knew he had to laugh to keep from crying.

Ms. Bridges would pick him up at eleven, and he needed to be packed and ready to go by ten. That would not be hard. The only earthly possessions Wes had were his well-worn Gideon Bible, some books and devotionals that had belonged to Preacher, and a radio. Wes just hadn't found the time to do much shopping while he had been at the McMarriott. The thought had occurred to him during the night that he did not own any other clothes. All Wes had were his prison-issue uniforms. Luckily, when he woke up, the guard had brought Wes a pair of jeans and a blue polo shirt. John said it was a gift from the warden.

After packing his things in a small plastic crate, Wes took off his prison clothes, folded them neatly, and laid them at the foot of his bed. He put on street clothes for the first time in five years. It felt almost uncomfortable, sort of like he was doing something wrong. When he was ready to go, he sat down on his bed for the last time and hung his head. The impact of what was happening hit him on the shoulders like a ton of bricks and fear rushed over him. He could feel himself start to tremble.

Dear God, I am truly, truly thankful for this opportunity. But I am scared. I don't want to mess up again. Please give me the strength every day to make the right decisions, one decision at a time. I want live for You, to bring glory to Your name. Thank you, thank you, thank you. In Jesus's name. Amen.

He took a deep breath and gathered himself. He looked up, and Bill said, "Time, buddy."

As Wes exited his cell for the last time, he stopped in the doorway and surveyed the bleak, gray cell that had been his home. *Never again.*

As Bill and Wes turned to walk down the hallway, the other prisoners gathered at their doors and scraped their tin cups against the bars in a show of respect. Even the prisoners who were not Jesus Freaks respected Wes for the way he had handled himself and the example he had set. The roar of the tin cups rattling against the jail bars was almost deafening. Wes shook hands with some of the prisoners as he passed by them and waved to the rest. He was fighting back tears and kept telling himself not to cry.

Bill led him to an office area where he had to sign some paperwork. In Greenwood, Wes would have to report to his parole officer at the courthouse on the first Monday of every month. No misses, no excuses. Wes listened intently, but he couldn't help glancing at the clock on the wall. For five years, time had been his worst enemy. Every day, he had fought against thinking about the clock and how much of that precious time he was wasting. His mind briefly jumped back to the time he had explained to Preacher what a time trial was. He laughed as he thought that his biggest, hardest time trial was coming to the end. *Getting stronger for what lays ahead,* he said. *God willing, hopefully I'll be ready.*

At five minutes to eleven, the secretary said, "Okay, I guess that does it."

How long he had waited for this moment, and now it was here.

The secretary gave him an understanding smile.

Could the second hand move any slower?

Bill touched him on the shoulder, smiled, and nodded toward the door.

Wes thanked the secretary, picked up his things, and headed for the door.

She smiled and said, "Good luck."

Bill led him down a short hallway and through a door he had never seen. Suddenly, Wes was standing in bright sunlight in a small, cement loading area enclosed by a tall brick wall with barbed wire on top. He raised his hand to shield the sun from his eyes as he shifted his crate under his left arm. He smiled as he saw most of the Jesus Freaks, the warden, and Ms. Bridges. Wes shook hands with each of the guys as they offered congratulations. He told each of them he would see them soon. He didn't linger because he was afraid his emotions would get the better of him.

At the end of the line, the warden extended his hand. "Good luck, son."

"Thank you, sir," Wes said.

"He's all yours, Ms. Bridges," the warden said.

She smiled at Wes as Bill escorted them to a series of doors on the opposite side of the loading area. After stepping through several doors, they were suddenly in a parking lot.

Patting him on the back, Bill said, "Take care of yourself, Wes."

"Will do. You too, Mr. Bill," Wes replied.

"I'm parked over here," Ms. Bridges said motioning to their left.

Wes froze in his tracks, taking in this glorious view of freedom on the outside of "The Wall."

"What's wrong?" she asked.

"Sorry, sorry," Wes replied. "Just can't believe it. It's so beautiful. Everything is pretty drab on the inside. I'm not used to seeing so much color. It's been so long."

"Let's get you out of here," she said with a laugh.

As they drove away, Wes couldn't help watching the prison get smaller and smaller in the rearview mirror. *Today is the first day of the rest of your life. Make it count.* "I just want to thank you, ma'am, for giving me a chance. I really do appreciate it," Wes said as they got out on Highway 378.

"First of all, let's get rid of some of the formality. You can call me Joan, okay?" she said.

"Sorry, no problem," Wes said.

"Secondly, as I said before, I really think this will be a win-win for both of us. Everything I have heard about you has been positive. Of course, I have read your file, and with all that's happened to you, I think you have something to offer our kids. They need a positive role model and lots of attention—and hearing it from someone who has made mistakes but learned from them will catch their attention."

"What exactly will I be doing?" Wes asked.

"Good question. I thought we could use this time to go over some things. As I said before, we typically have fifteen or so kids. They usually are under thirteen years of age, mainly because older kids are harder to deal with because they are maturing sexually. In a home with boys and girls, that can cause some problems. We usually have boys and girls in middle school or below. They go to school during the day, and we pick them up afterward. That's where you come in. We have a female counselor for the girls. Her name is Roxie. And you will be the boys' counselor. You will need to be there after school Monday through Friday from three till nine. You and Roxie will organize activities for them, help them with homework and supper, and get them to bed. We have folks who stay overnight, and we have weekend folks who stay Saturday and Sunday. I know you need a few more hours to graduate, and I thought you could get those classes in the mornings. How's all this sounding so far?"

"Too good to be true. Can I ask one question," Wes replied. "You, I mean, we are a Christian organization. Are we permitted to talk about the Bible with them?"

"That's another reason we chose you, Wes. I know you have been important to the prison ministry. We were hoping you could use that with the kids. Are you comfortable with that?"

"Absolutely," Wes said. "Same message, different audience."

"Very good," Joan replied. "Let's see, what else. Oh yeah, pay. You will get paid ten dollars per hour. I hope that's okay?"

"Are you kidding? I feel like I already won the lottery," Wes said with a laugh. "You guys have done so much for me already. I just hope I can help these kids. I definitely will do the best I can."

"You will. I'm sure," she replied. "The best thing you can give these kids is attention. They are starving for it."

After a few minutes, Joan said, "We are almost to town. Have you been to Greenwood before?"

"Yes. I ran cross-country in high school, and we ran against Emerald here once. I think it was at a children's home, which is kind of ironic now."

"That would have been Connie Maxwell. It will be right up here on the right. A few of our kids end up there for long-term placements. We will go by your house first to let you see it, and then I'll take you to meet everyone. Your house is a few blocks from Bower-Rodgers. If you want, you can pick out a bike from our supply to get around."

"Sure, thanks," Wes replied. "Can I ask one other question?"

Joan nodded.

"What will people think of my record? I mean, how much do they know?"

"We've had other people doing their community service with us. As far as I'm concerned, that's all this is. I've told the ones who needed to know that you were someone the court system decided to give another chance. The details are yours to share if and when you choose. How does that sound?"

"Good. Thank you," Wes replied.

As they reached a residential area, Joan said, "Here we are— 216 Jennings Avenue. It's this pretty little house over here on the right. This is a quiet, older section of town. Distinctive houses. It's a great place to run, by the way, and downtown is just a couple of blocks away."

They pulled up to a small brick house with green shutters and a swing on the porch. A huge oak tree in the front yard shaded the entire house. Wes looked at the house and the tree like he had never seen something so wonderful. The smell of boxwoods was in the air. Wes glanced at the big house next door to see boxwoods lining the front walkway.

As they walked up to the porch, Joan said, "Let's see what the inside looks like." She opened the door to reveal a small, beige den furnished with a brown couch, several chairs, and a TV on a stand.

Expecting to see a vacant room, Wes laughed out loud. "Wow, this is for me?"

"We all pitched in to help furnish it for you. I know it's not much, but hopefully it will be comfortable," Joan started to say.

"Are you kidding? This is the Taj Mahal compared to where I've been." He moved on to the hallway to take a quick look in the two bedrooms. One was unfurnished, but the other had a bed and a chest of drawers. Towels hung in the small bathroom at the end of the hall. On the kitchen table, he was shocked to see a watermelon, a box of candy, and several books and magazines.

"This is way too much. I don't know what to say." Wes shook his head and picked up the book.

"It's a Charles Stanley devotional. Are you familiar with him?" Joan asked.

"Oh, yes. He is one of my favorites. I love listening to him preach on the radio."

"Good," Joan said. "We also got you several running magazines. And check out the fridge and cabinets. I don't think I mentioned it, but we have a resale store where people can donate used items, and we can sell them to raise money to operate the home. You have a hundred-dollar credit there to get whatever you need—clothes or things for the house."

Wes opened the refrigerator, and it was stocked with milk, juice, Gatorade, ketchup, and mustard. "Wow." The cabinets revealed an even bigger bounty of canned goods, bread, cereal, and cooking supplies. "I don't know what to say. Thank you so much. All this for somebody like me? It's way too much."

"Wes, you need to let that go right now. We all make mistakes. Some are just more visible," Joan said. "The slate is clean, okay?"

"I know. I just worry about how I will be received. With a record and everything," Wes said.

"Well, we believe in a God of second chances, and you know what Romans 8:28 tells us. As I said, it's up to you to tell as little or as much as you desire."

"You are beginning to sound like Preacher," Wes said with a laugh.

"Preacher? I think I'd like to hear more about him sometime," Joan said. "How about we go meet your coworkers now?"

"Sure," Wes said.

Two blocks down West Cambridge Street, they arrived at the Bowers-Rodgers Home, which was on a short dead-end street. It was an older, two-story white house with signs of children everywhere—a playground, bikes, toys, and a basketball goal. It was separated from a smaller white building by a parking lot.

Joan pointed to the smaller building as they got out of the car. "Those are our offices, and on the back side, there is an activity room. Let's go in the big house to see what's for lunch."

They entered the back door, and two ladies were busily preparing deli sandwiches in the kitchen.

Another lady entered the room and said, "Hello, Wes. I'm Susan. I'm the house coordinator. This is Robbie, our first shift mom, and Gayle is one of our devoted volunteers."

They all said hello.

Susan said, "We're glad to have you. Would you like to have lunch with us?"

Wes turned to Joan as if waiting permission.

"Of course we would," Joan said with a laugh.

After a nice lunch with the ladies and several toddlers, Joan continued their tour of the home. In the basement, clothes were separated and stored for children of all ages. In the front of the house, there were two dens—one for smaller children and one with two computers, games, and a television for older kids. There was a cozy nursery with six cribs. The four upstairs bedrooms had alarms on the doors so the evening mom would know if anyone tried to leave during the night.

Throughout the tour, Joan described the types of families and situations the kids came from.

Wes looked out one of the bedroom windows and noticed a big fenced playground.

Joan said, "Wes, I am so sorry. How thoughtless of me. I've just been chattering on. We can do this later. I'm sure there are other things you would rather do today than listen to me. Where can I take you?"

Wes smiled sheepishly, "Ma'am, if it's okay, I think I'd just like to go for a long run and walk around town maybe. I'd like to get some fresh air, if that's okay? It's been a while."

"Of course," Joan said. "I'll take you back to your house and leave you to yourself. Supper is at six. I will pick you up a few minutes before that so you can meet Roxie and the kids. How is that?"

"Sounds great," Wes said with a smile.

CHAPTER 18

WELCOME

Wes Strong had never run so much just for the pure fun and enjoyment of it. He ran some, walked some, and smiled a lot. No concern for pace, distance, or time. It had been five years since he had been able to run in complete freedom. No walls or barriers. So much had changed—cars, clothes—but everything looked beautiful.

Wes tried not to stare at things, but he couldn't help himself: a red bird in a tree, bright lights in a store, multicolored impatiens, children in strollers. It was like he was really seeing his surroundings for the first time. The colors were so vivid. Even the sky was bluer. Wes had no idea how far he ran, but he covered as much of the town as he could. He lost track of time, and it was five thirty before he knew it. He sprinted back to his house and took a quick shower.

Wes had just finished dressing and was tying his shoes when he heard doors slamming in front of his house. He looked out to see a light blue van with kids pouring out of it. Before he could reach the door, the doorbell was ringing nonstop. Children were laughing on the porch.

When Wes opened the door, two small girls were holding a tray of chocolate chip cookies above their heads. "Surprise," they exclaimed.

Several boys and other girls jumped onto the porch, all blurting out questions at one time.

"Thank you," Wes said as he took the tray.

The last person onto the porch was a blonde, athletic-looking girl about the same age as Wes. "Hi," she said. "I'm Roxie, and this is our crew. They wanted to surprise you. They talked Joan into letting them bring you cookies. These two with the cookies are Faith and Julia. They are five and six, and they are sisters. This guy over here is their big brother Rob. He is nine. This young lady is Sheeka and she is eight. And this is her twin brother Ty. And these two young guys are Paul who is six and Tim who is seven. Everybody say hello to Wes."

They burst out laughing and yelled, "Hello to Wes!"

"Wow. Thank you, guys," Wes replied with a smile.

"Who's ready for supper?" Roxie asked.

"Me!" They all poured back into the van.

"Everything revolves around food." Roxie smiled. "You ready?"

"Sure." Wes put down the cookies and shut the door.

Once they were all loaded in the van, Ty asked Wes if he had ever played soccer.

Wes replied that he had played a little when he was younger.

"Good," Ty responded. "You're on our team. Boys against girls after supper. Okay, Roxie?"

"I don't know," Roxie said with a smile. "You sure you guys want to lose again?"

"Yeah," Sheeka said. "You guys don't stand a chance—even with Wes. Roxie is the best, and you know it."

"We'll see," all the guys blurted out.

During a rowdy supper of spaghetti and salad, Wes was overwhelmed by all the activity. All he could do was watch in amazement at all the noise and kids running around. It definitely was different than the order and discipline of prison life. Most of the kids talked nonstop about anything and everything, especially Ty.

Roxie smiled at Wes and said, "You'll get used to it. It's pretty crazy at first. We've got a pretty young group right now, which is probably good to break you in with. They crave attention, but at least there is not too much drama with them. Not yet, anyway."

Afterward, everyone gathered on the playground behind the house where there were two small soccer goals set up about twenty yards apart. The kids continued to chatter nonstop. The excitement picked up as the sugar kicked in from the cookies.

Ty grabbed Wes by the hand and said, "Come on down here. You're with us." Turning his attention to the girls dancing in circles at the other end, Ty said, "Bring it on, turkeys!"

With a whoop and a holler, the game began. The boys chased the ball all over the field like wild banshees. It was more like organized chaos than soccer.

Roxie was the best player on the field and used her skills to keep possession of the ball. She was playing keep-away from the boys and was not really trying to score, but periodically she would dribble close enough to the goal to let one of the girls take a shot.

Wes ran around quietly with the guys, trying to get the hang of things. They were chasing and kicking the ball wildly and not really trying to pass to each other.

After the girls scored two goals without the boys even getting off a shot, Wes said, "Time-out. Come here, guys."

As the boys gathered, they were grumbling about how bad they were and how it was not fair.

Wes said, "Listen guys. We've got to get organized and spread out. Everybody can't chase the ball at one time. Have you ever heard of Joshua in the Bible?"

The boys shook their heads and wondered what that had to do with their soccer game.

Wes said, "Well, Joshua was a great general who led the Israelites into the Promised Land. He listened to God and learned how to organize his troops. So we're going to do like them and organize." He positioned the boys at certain points on the field and told them to stay in their areas and not run all over the field. "When you get the ball, look for a teammate to pass to. Okay?"

As the game restarted, the boys did as Wes had instructed and quickly scored a goal.

"Good job, guys," Wes said. "See what happens when you spread out?"

The boys continued to follow Wes's instructions, and slowly their play improved.

Wes was impressed with how well they all played together and how much fun they were all having. He couldn't help thinking about where he had been twenty-four hours earlier. *What a difference a day makes.*

The ball scooted loose close to him, and Wes started to dribble toward the goal for an open shot.

Roxie came up from behind and stole the ball. She laughed as all the girls let out a yell of approval. Finally, after several minutes of playing keep-away from the boys, Ty was able to get possession of the ball and passed it to Tim who was able to score. It wouldn't have happened if Wes had not shielded Roxie from the ball.

"Good teamwork, guys," Wes said as the boys celebrated.

"Okay," Roxie said, "I think that's enough. Time to get ready for bed."

The boys yelled, "That's the first time we've tied them. Yeah."

As the kids filed into the house, Roxie said, "Good job with the guys, Wes. I like the way you worked Joshua into the game. I don't think I've ever seen that done."

"Thanks," Wes replied. "You're really good. You've played before?"

"Yeah, growing up, in high school, and some during college at Lander."

"Wow. It shows," Wes said.

After the kids were ready for bed, Roxie asked if Wes would like to read a bedtime story to those who were interested.

"Sure," Wes said. "How about I tell a story instead?"

"Sounds good," Roxie replied.

Wes said, "You remember how I mentioned Joshua while we were playing soccer? Well, let me tell you how he led the Israelites to conquer the walled city of Jericho." He recounted how God had told Joshua to have the Israelites walk around the walled city once a day for six days, and then on the seventh day, they walked around it seven times while blowing their trumpets. Then, the walls fell, and the Israelites conquered the city. "So, the point of the story, guys, is that good things always happen when we do what God tells us to do. Does that make sense?"

"Like we did playing soccer?" Ty asked.

"In everything," Wes said with a laugh. "Okay, I think it's time for bed. I had a really good time with you guys today. Thanks for bringing me cookies too."

"Nice job, Wes. I think we may have to keep you around," Roxie said after making sure the kids were all settled in for the night. "Let me give you a ride back to your house."

"Thanks, but if it's okay, I think I'll walk tonight. I just want to take it all in. It's been a big day."

"I understand." She smiled and waved good-bye.

Walking home under the streetlights, Wes realized it had been five years since he had seen stars or the moon. The beautiful crescent moon was surrounded by millions of stars. As he strolled along, all he could think about was a verse from Psalms he had read that morning in his devotional: "The moon and the stars to rule over the night, for His steadfast love endures forever."

Absolutely. Absolutely. His steadfast love endures forever. Wes walked slowly down West Cambridge Street toward Jennings Avenue, bathed in moonlight and enjoying the sweet taste of freedom.

CHAPTER 19

THE STARTING LINE

The next morning, Wes woke up at six without setting his alarm. It had become so ingrained in his system over the last five years. He raised his head and looked around for a minute before he remembered where he was. *So it wasn't a dream*, he thought.

He slid out of bed with a big smile and dropped to his knees beside his bed. He gave thanks to God for delivering him from prison and for giving him a second chance. After eating a quick bowl of cereal, he went on another long run just to take in more of his new surroundings. It was like he was seeing so many things for the first time. His senses were so heightened. The sounds of the birds chirping, the smell of freshly cut grass, even the air felt new—lighter. While he was out, he stopped by the Bowers-Rodgers Home to see what time he should report to work.

"Hey, Wes," Joan said with a big smile. "I heard everything went really well last night. What did you think?"

"It was fantastic, ma'am. One of the best days of my life, definitely. The kids were a lot of fun."

"Big change, I bet," Joan said.

"Yes, no doubt. But actually similar in some ways." Wes smiled. "I didn't mean to interrupt your work, but I just wanted to see if you needed me to come in any earlier today."

"That would be good. If you want, you can come at twelve thirty for lunch, and then we can do that paperwork."

"See you then," Wes replied.

When Wes returned for lunch, the morning ladies gave him another big welcome.

Joan was at the table, feeding a baby out of several jars. "Hey, Wes," she said. "Fix a plate and make yourself at home."

He fixed a plate and sat beside Joan.

She said, "I heard a funny story about you from your neighbors already."

Wes frowned in response, curious about what he had done.

"One of our volunteers lives on your street, and she said it looked like Chip Marvin was back in town."

The other ladies giggled at the mention of this name.

Wes looked around curiously. "Chip Marvin?"

Joan smiled. "Well, every town has its local characters, and Chip was definitely a character. He came from a wealthy family and lived in a house down the street from you. Local legend has it that he was a brilliant student along the lines of Einstein. Shortly after graduating from college, he had a nervous breakdown and was never the same. He ran around town for years and years, telling everyone and anyone that he was a professor at Lander. He was a quirky, thin little guy, and he ran everywhere without a shirt, showing off his ribs. Very distinctive person. Wanda saw you running and said you reminded her of Chip."

Wes smiled. "I'll be sure to keep my shirt on then. Is he still around?"

Joan frowned and shook her head, "No, no. Unfortunately, he was murdered several years back by a guy doing yard work at his house. Very sad. I think Greenwood lost its innocence when that happened."

"Oh, wow," Wes replied. "That's terrible."

After lunch and filing out the necessary W-2 forms, Roxie arrived.

Wes rode with her in the van to pick up the kids from school. They went to three different elementary schools to gather the flock. The kids were all surprised but excited to see Wes, especially Ty. He was definitely enjoying having a man around. After the kids were all together, Ty asked if they could go to the civic center.

"Exactly what I was thinking," Roxie replied.

The kids let out a yell of approval.

"We need to show it to Wes," Roxie said. "The civic center had sports fields, a large playground, and a walking/running track. It's a big treat for the kids to get to go there. They all love it because there is something for everyone."

"Sounds good to me," Wes agreed.

After stopping by the home to drop off their book bags and have a snack, they were off to the civic center playground. It was a perfect spring day.

The kids made Wes try out all the playground equipment, including the swings, the climbing bars, and the seesaw.

After playing on the playground for about thirty minutes, Wes asked Roxie if he could take some of the kids for a run around the track. The playground was in the middle of the play area, and the track on the perimeter could be seen at all times.

"I heard you were a runner," Roxie replied. "Go for it."

Wes called all the kids around and said, "Who wants to take a run around the track with me?"

The guys were all for it, but the only girl who wanted to go was Sheeka. The rest of the girls were happy to stay on the playground with Roxie.

"Okay, guys, one slow lap with me," Wes said as they gathered on the track. Wes started out in front of the group, but Ty and the other boys took off like wild animals. Wes let them go for a minute to exhaust them before calling for them to wait. They stopped and waited, doubled over and gasping for air. "Okay, guys. We are doing an easy run and not a sprint. There is a difference. If you can't run and talk to me, then you are running too fast. Understand? Let's stay together and take it easy. Why don't each of you tell me what your favorite subject is while we run? Can you do that?"

Wes was able to keep the guys together for the rest of that lap and tried to keep the conversation going to slow them down. "Much better, guys," Wes said as they arrived back at the playground. "Remember the story I told you about Joshua and how they marched around Jericho? Well, you guys just marched around our Jericho. Right?"

"Does that mean we captured the playground?" Ty asked.

"I guess so," Wes replied.

"Yeah, we captured the girls."

Wes looked at Roxie and shook his head. "Well, at least they remembered the story," he said with a smile.

Wes's first month of freedom flew by. He continued to soak up the newness of everything. For the first several Saturday mornings, Joan drove Wes back to McCormick to visit with the guys at the McMarriott. He was allowed two hours with his friends. The guys needed to see him succeeding, and he needed to continue to minister to them.

Wes felt like the group had saved his life even if Preacher was no longer there. Preacher's spirit was definitely alive and well. It was an uplifting time for all involved. They fellowshipped and caught up on news inside and outside the prison. Wes was happy to hear that Big Frank and Wolf were leading devotionals now during the week, and Watts was holding true to his word and taking a turn at preaching to the guys.

On the way back from his fourth trip, Wes told Joan how much he appreciated her transporting him to McCormick.

She said, "Actually, I have been working on that, and I think I have some good news. You know how I said we have a resale store?"

Wes nodded and listened closely. He had learned that when Joan had good news, it usually meant *very good* news.

"Once in awhile, someone will donate a car to us to resell, and we just received an older Honda Civic. I've talked to our board, and they agreed to let me sell it to you for eight hundred dollars. You can pay it off by working at the resale store from twelve to three during the week. We always need help there with sorting, unloading, and stocking. Would you be interested in that?"

"Wow! Thank you. That sounds great," Wes stammered. "You guys have done so much for me already. I don't know what to say."

"You're welcome," Joan replied. "Just keep up the good work. This will give you a way to get back and forth to McCormick. Also, in the fall, they will work with you at the store so you can take the classes you need at Lander."

"Definitely. I've been checking into that, and I think it will work out fine. Hopefully, I will qualify for a student loan." Wes continued to be amazed at how God had blessed him. Everything was coming together better than he could have ever imagined, and he was so thankful for his second chance. The kids were taking to him, and he was getting comfortable with them. Roxie was easy to work with, and all the folks at the Bowers-Rodgers Home made him feel like part of the family. He was able to run in the mornings, work at the resale store in the early afternoons, and go to the home at three to be with the kids. But as summer began, he was about to face his first real test.

All of the original kids were still there, with the exception of Paul, whose grandmother had gained custody of him. One Saturday evening, they received Jose, a small Hispanic twelve-year-old who had just seen his drunken father assaulting his mother. The neighbors called the police who arrested his father and took his mother to the hospital. She had been admitted with broken ribs and possible internal injuries. DSS had brought Jose to Bowers-Rodgers late in the evening.

When Wes arrived on Monday afternoon, Roxie filled him in on Jose, and she told him that Jose was having some pretty serious anger issues. He had pushed some of the other kids around and was not cooperating with the counselor. Bowers-Rodgers had a grant to fund a part-time counselor, and Nikki was there to help the kids get through rough times.

Wes looked out the window as Roxie talked. Jose was kicking the soccer ball into the goal. He had his hands on the crossbar about three feet off the ground, and he continuously kicked the ball as hard as he could into the net. Wes asked Roxie if it was all right if he talked to him.

"Sure," Roxie said. "Good luck."

As Wes walked out onto the playground, Jose never lifted his head or stopped his angry task. "Hey, Jose. I'm Wes. I help out here in the afternoons."

Without really listening or giving Wes a chance to continue, Jose said, "I don't want to be here. Why do I have to stay here?"

"Well, you know there are some things going on with your parents, and your mom is in the hospital for a little while to make sure she is okay. You're here while those things get worked out. I promise we'll take good care of you and do some fun things. Okay? But I need you to be nice to everybody. All right?"

Jose nodded slowly without looking up.

Wes patted him on the back. "You hungry? I sure am. I saw they have some chicken fingers and French fries inside. How about I bring some out for us?"

"Okay," Jose said.

Food always opens doors, Wes thought as he headed inside.

He and Jose sat outside and talked as they ate. Jose answered some of Wes's questions about school and sports. He liked soccer a lot and didn't care for school very much. Wes told him that was okay because he didn't care for school a lot either at his age. And Wes told him that he liked to run, but that he was not very good at soccer.

"Roxie, the other counselor here, is a really good soccer player though. She played in college. We play almost every night. Would you like that?"

Finally making eye contact with Wes, Jose said, "Yeah. Can we play tonight?"

"I don't think that would be a problem."

Over the next few days, Jose's behavior slowly improved as he got more comfortable with the other kids and Wes. Wes tried to pay him extra attention, and it seemed to be helping. Jose asked every day how his mother was doing and if he could see her. After four days, the news came that she was going to require surgery the next day to repair some damage to one of her kidneys. Jose did not take the news very well, but it helped when Wes told him they could visit her that night.

The next afternoon, Roxie and Wes took the kids to the civic center to play. While playing soccer, Jose and Ty got into an argument, and Jose knocked Ty to the ground.

Wes jumped in and separated them quickly. "Let's go for a walk, Jose," Wes said and motioned toward the track. "Look, Jose, I know things are not good right now, but you've got to get control of that temper before it gets you into trouble. Things will get better."

"What do you know? " Jose replied.

Wes replied, "More than you think, buddy. I've been in your shoes. I know how rough it can be."

"Right," Jose responded sarcastically.

Wes was in unfamiliar territory. He knew the day was coming when his past would collide with the present, but he didn't want it to be today. He was not sure what words to choose. He wanted to be able to help the kids, but he wasn't sure how much information he wanted to give out about his own past. He thought for a second before he touched Jose on the shoulder and turned to face him. "Jose, I've seen my dad hit my mom too. He had a bad temper, and he took it out on us. This was before there was a home like Bowers-Rodgers, so we couldn't leave. I was too young to do anything about it, but it made me angry a lot too. That's when I started running more. I ran because I was so mad and couldn't change things and because my Dad was pretty mean to me. I just wanted to scream at the top of my lungs. Do you know what I mean?"

Jose nodded.

Wes said, "In high school, I learned how to use that anger to make me a good runner. At first, I ran hard because I was so mad, but then I learned that I could use that anger in a positive way to make me a better runner. You need to learn the same thing. You have to find a positive way to use that anger. I know it's hard, but we have to learn to trust God. He will work things out. Do you understand?"

Jose kicked at the ground.

"Tell you what," Wes said. "Let's me and you take a jog the rest of the way around this track, okay?" Wes took off, looked back over his shoulder, and said, "Come on, dude."

Jose looked up and ran to catch up.

"That's it—but not too fast. We're not sprinting. Just chilling."

They made their way around the track and back to the playground where the others were.

Wes said, "Nice job. That helps, doesn't it?"

Jose said, "Yeah, I guess so."

Jose continued to have good days and bad days, and Wes continued to talk to him about controlling his anger.

Wes and Roxie planned group activities to encourage Jose to get along with the others. Jose genuinely seemed to be trying, and Wes felt encouraged. It was tough for Wes and Roxie to share their attention evenly among their charges, especially with a different child needing to be the center of attention each day, but they did the best they could.

It was always good to go to the civic center. Wes continued to take the interested kids on short runs around the track. He had succeeded in getting all the kids to try it at different times, even the girls.

When Wes got to work the next day, Roxie said, "I have an idea. On Saturday, there is a 5K race and a fun run uptown. The fun run is about a fourth of a mile. Don't you think our kids could handle that? I thought it might be fun for them, and I think they get a medal and a T-shirt for participating. I know the organizer, and I think he would let them run for free. What do you think?"

"That's a great idea. I was hoping to do something like that eventually. It might really be encouraging to them and give them a sense of accomplishment, especially Jose," Wes said.

"Great. I'll take care of it," Roxie replied.

Saturday morning was cool but bright and sunny. *Perfect for running*, Wes thought as he pulled into the Bowers-Rodgers parking lot.

Roxie was loading the kids into the van. They had been talking about the race ever since Wes and Roxie broke the news to them. Even Jose seemed to be looking forward to it.

Ty said, "Hey, Wes., I'm going to win a medal. Let's go, man."

Wes waved and said, "You guys all ready? What are you waiting for?"

"You!" they yelled.

The race was starting at the big water fountain on the square. The fun run would take place thirty minutes before the 5K.

Wes said, "Okay, guys. Let's do a little warm-up jog over to that building and back."

Roxie handed out race bibs with official running numbers that they pinned to their shirts to make them feel like real runners.

The officials made the announcement for everyone to head to the start line for the fun run.

Wes told the kids that it was just an easy run—and to not knock anyone down. The gun sounded, and they were on their way. Wes jogged behind the group. The fun run was just a big circle around the outside of the fountain parking lot, but it might as well have been the Olympics to those kids. Everyone finished with big smiles, and nobody fell down. Jose and Ty finished near the front.

"Way to go, guys," Wes exclaimed. "Give me five. Good job, everybody."

Everyone shared smiles, especially when they got their medals. "See my medal, Wes. I never got a medal before," Ty exclaimed.

"I see. I see," Wes replied. "I'm proud of all you guys. Y'all want to stick around and watch the other race?"

"Yes, they do," Roxie replied as she handed Wes a running bib.

"What's this?" Wes asked.

"The kids want to see you race. I signed you up," she replied.

"Oh, I don't know. It's been a while," Wes said, shaking his head.

The kids said, "Please, Wes. That's the other reason we wanted to come. Roxie said to keep it secret so we could surprise you. Come on. Do it for us."

"Well, okay," Wes said. "Let me stretch a little and warm up, but don't expect much."

Wes ran around the block and did some twenty-yard sprints beside the Grier Building, the six-story office building that dominated the downtown landscape.

As the announcer called out five minutes to start, Wes did a few more quick stretches and retied his shoes with double knots.

Roxie tapped him on the shoulder and pointed to a tall, skinny kid with long legs and a Lander University singlet. "There's your competition. He runs for Lander."

"Oh, yeah." Wes glanced over and said, "I doubt that. I don't think he has anything to worry about."

"Good luck, Wes," the kids yelled as he moved to the start line.

Wes had thought about eventually racing again, but it hadn't been a big priority. He had told himself his running life was in the past. He wanted to concentrate on making a difference in these kids' lives and making the most of his second chance. Running competitively can be a selfish, lonely endeavor, and he wanted to prove that he was a different person now—one who was focused on helping others and serving God.

It's not about me anymore. One race won't hurt though. It might be fun to see how I measure up after almost six years—and if makes the kids happy, then why not?

When the gun went off, Wes told himself not to go out too fast. *Just tuck in behind somebody, see how you feel, and see how it feels to be in a race again.*

The Lander runner went out fast, and a pack of about five other runners, including Wes, stayed back about ten yards. They headed down South Main Street, which was a slight downhill. With the adrenaline pumping, it was hard to hold back and not go out too fast. *Take it easy.* Wes had to keep telling himself to get his breathing under control. *Boy, I'm rusty.*

As they turned onto Alexander Street to loop around the hospital on the south side of town, several of the other runners began to fade. The Lander runner stayed about ten yards in front of Wes and the thinning pack. *He's probably on cruise control,* Wes thought as his breathing labored on. He didn't have a watch on and had no idea what pace they were running as they passed the one-mile mark and the first water station. It felt pretty fast, and it stayed that way as they made several right turns around Self Memorial Hospital.

After the last turn onto Spring Street, Wes realized the other two guys had fallen off. He had picked up a couple of yards on the lead runner in his Lander royal blue. *This is interesting,* Wes thought. When he guessed they had less than a mile left, he decided to hang tight for a second. *I sure would like to finish strong for the kids.*

Another voice entered his head from out of the blue. Preacher said, "Run for me."

For a second, he was back in the rec yard and holding his dying friend's hand. That was all it took to give him a second wind and a new purpose. Wes closed the gap quickly on the lead runner who, glancing over his shoulder, suddenly realized he had some competition.

At the finish area, Roxie and the kids had climbed the steps of an office building. It offered a perfect perch to see down the street since the balcony completely circled the two-story stucco building. It overlooked Spring Street and the final turn to the finish line.

As the Lander runner turned onto Spring Street, Roxie said, "Look, guys, here comes the first runner." Another runner was tucked in behind him, but she couldn't tell who it was. When she realized it was Wes, she jumped in the air and yelled, "Guys, guys. It's Wes. Yell for Wes."

The kids were running back and forth on the balcony and having fun, but when they saw Roxie jumping up and down, they went crazy. "Go, Wes, go," they yelled.

Wes was in the zone and could not hear them. He was focused on the task at hand, which was getting past the lanky runner just several feet ahead of him. One more turn and then a thirty-yard sprint to the finish. He was pretty sure this guy would have a strong kick at the finish, but Wes decided to try something he had learned from Batman and Robin in high school. He fell off his target by a couple of steps to make him think he had faded.

When the Lander runner made the final turn to the right and instinctively glanced over his right shoulder to see how far back his competition was, Wes sprinted past him on his left. It happened so fast and unexpectedly that Wes was several yards ahead by the time the leader responded. The sprint to the finish was on.

Wes gave it everything he had. He knew the Lander runner would not go down without a fight, and he would have to push it. The finish line could not get there quickly enough, and Wes clipped the tape just ahead of his shocked opponent.

The kids were jumping up and down and screaming, "He won. He won. Wes won."

Wes touched his chest, pointed to the heavens, and doubled over. As he gasped for breath, the Lander runner came over and said. "Good job. I'm Tim Atkins."

Wes introduced himself and said, "That was a very tough run."

"Where are you from?" Tim asked.

"Walhalla, but I live here now," Wes said.

"Okay, see you around," Tim said.

When the kids reached Wes, he smiled and high-fived all of them.

Roxie ran up and said, "Wes, I had no idea you were that fast. I was just kidding at the start. Tim is the conference champion. He hasn't lost a race in two years. Wow!"

"Really?" Wes glanced at the official race clock, which had been stopped at the winning time: 15:38. It was twelve seconds off his personal best. *Wow. That's interesting.*

CHAPTER 20

WARRIORS

When Wes reported to work on Monday, Susan said that Joan wanted to see him. *I wonder what's up,* he thought as he walked across the parking lot to Joan's office. In his brief time there, he had learned that he did not have anything to fear when he was summoned to her office. In fact, Joan had blessed him with so many gifts that he had come to look forward to being summoned to see her. It was more like going to see Santa than being sent to the principal's office.

"Hello," Wes said as he tapped on her door.

"Hey." Joan looked up from her paperwork. "Come on in."

Wes sat down in front of her chair.

Joan said, "I hear congratulations are in order. Roxie said you are quite a runner."

"Thanks. No one was as surprised as I was—I promise you. It's been a while." Wes smiled. "I hope that was okay."

"Absolutely. I just wanted to let you know that I am very proud of you and want to encourage you to keep it up. These kids need to have somebody to look up to, and when they see you do well, it's such a lift to them. It's the first thing several of them told me about this morning. They were so excited to get to run and get those medals and see you win. There's so much negative in their lives that they need all the positives they can get. I'm sure it's the same with your friends in McCormick."

"Thanks a bunch," Wes replied. "I'm glad to hear you say that. Actually, I have been thinking about that and wanted to run something by you. As you know, running can be such a positive in kid's lives—both physically and psychologically. If it's okay with you, I'd like to continue to encourage the kids here to run. Nothing formal or required. I just want to introduce them to it and maybe give them an outlet down the road for some of their energy if nothing else. It's a great way to burn off some frustration, let me tell you. I also was wondering if there might be some money available to print some T-shirts that say 'Warriors for Christ' on the front and maybe have a picture of a runner on there and a Bible verse on the back. They would get one if they agree to run with me. I talked to them some about Joshua and his warriors, so I thought they could be Wes's Warriors. The Bible verse I had in mind is Jeremiah 20:11. 'The Lord is with me like a mighty Warrior.'"

"Wes, that is a wonderful idea. Absolutely," Joan replied. "I'm sure we can get a good deal on some shirts. What color were you thinking?"

"Definitely something bright—maybe yellow?"

"I'll take care of it," Joan said. "Thanks again for all you are doing."

When the kids were playing on the playground, Wes told Roxie about his conversation with Joan.

Roxie said, "You never know what seeds we plant here that might sprout into something really good in these kids' lives down the road. I think the shirts would mean a lot to them. It will give them a sense of belonging and importance. A lot of them have never had that."

"Yeah," Wes replied. "I just know it was good for me after I got past the negatives in my life. I hope it will be similar for them."

Roxie asked, "How did it feel on Saturday?"

"It was interesting. It had been so long, almost like in another life. I had pretty much written off competing again. It felt really good to be out there again. Thank you for giving me that push. I just don't want it to take over. It's not a priority now. I don't know," Wes said.

"Hey." Roxie tapped his arm to bring him back to the present. "Did you see how excited the kids were? They absolutely loved it. It means a lot to them when they see you do well."

"Yeah, that's what Joan said," Wes replied. "I feel really blessed to be here, and I don't want anything to distract me from our work. Competing can make you self-centered and obsessive if you're not careful."

"I understand completely," Roxie replied. "I don't know how much you know about it, but I used to struggle with some eating issues. It got to the point where I could not compete in sports because I just did not have the energy. I was too caught up in it and thinking I needed to eat less to stay thin to see what was going on. It was a vicious cycle. I know what you mean about being afraid it will take over."

"You look healthy now. How did you get through it?"

"After I stopped playing soccer, I started going to a group counseling session at school. Some of the girls encouraged me to go to Anthony's Bible study at First Baptist. It was such an eye opener. I quickly learned that it's not about me—it's about Him. It really helped me get my focus off myself and start looking outward. There are so many hurting people in the world, especially kids, who need help and need to hear about Christ. And here I am."

"Wow," Wes said.

"My point is that you can still compete to bring glory to Him and be a positive role model to these kids. God might have bigger plans for your running than letting it become self-centered. It can be Christ-centered. Let's keep each other accountable on our issues, okay?"

"Deal." Wes smiled back at her.

Wes felt like he had found his place in the world and his purpose in life. He continued to thank God every day for his new chance and tried to make the most of his opportunity at Bowers-Rodgers. Summer was flying by, and the kids were coming and going. Some stayed for a few days before they were released to family members, and others stayed for months while the judicial system churned along at a snail's pace.

Ty was gone, but Jose was still there while his mother recuperated from surgery. He had shown much improvement in his attitude and temper. Wes played a large part and saw a little of himself in Jose. The boy seemed to be enjoying running with Wes and was proud of his Warrior T-shirt.

Four weeks after the 5K, Roxie told Wes there would be another one the following Saturday. When they told the kids, Jose asked if he could run.

Wes looked at Roxie and said, "I don't see why not."

Roxie agreed.

"Will you run too, Wes?" Jose asked.

Roxie said, "You bet he will."

Wes continued to run in the mornings and added more speed work to his regimen. He was feeling pretty good about his conditioning. He couldn't help wondering if Tim would be there. He knew he would want revenge. Wes wouldn't be able to surprise him again.

When they arrived on Saturday, Tim was nowhere to be seen.

Wes and Roxie took the kids to the fun run, and they were so excited about their T-shirts and medals.

Jose and Wes warmed up together before the 5K. After several sprints, Wes said, "Jose, what is the most important thing to remember during the race?"

"Don't start out too fast?"

Wes shook his head. "Yes, but there's something more important than that."

Jose frowned.

Wes said, "Just have fun, dude."

They laughed and high-fived each other.

Without Tim there, Wes easily won the 5K. As soon as he finished, he jogged back out onto the course to cheer on Jose.

Several hundred yards back on the course, Jose was sprinting along with a huge smile on his face.

"Looking good, Jose," Wes yelled. "Finish strong."

Jose won the under-fifteen-group. He didn't stop smiling for the rest of the day and carried the small trophy he received around everywhere.

A few weeks later, Jose's mother was released from the hospital. His father was still in jail and probably would remain there.

When the day came for Jose to rejoin his mother, he and Wes took a walk together. Wes told him how proud he was of him and said he would be there if Jose needed him. "Will you keep running?" Wes asked.

"Oh yeah," Jose said.

"Good," Wes replied. "Let's run together sometime. I hope you'll try out for cross-country this year. I think you will do well. And when you get angry, just go for a run and talk to God. Pour if out to Him like we've talked about before and give it to Him. He can handle it. I promise. He loves you, and I do too."

Wes gave him a hug, and Jose was soon gone. Wes said a prayer for him as he watched him disappear out of the parking lot. Wes turned his attention back to the other kids on the playground.

Roxie came out and said, "Do you think Jose will be okay?"

"I hope so. I'm sure going to pray for him."

Roxie said, "Me too. How'd you like to go to Greenville next month and take the kids to a race up there? I thought we could take them to the zoo too. Joan said it would be fine."

"Sounds good," Wes replied. "Another 5K would be fun."

Roxie said, "It's not just a 5K."

Wes looked at her. "10K?"

Shaking her head sheepishly, she said, "No."

"You're kidding. What then?"

"Half-marathon," she said slyly.

"Are you crazy?" Wes laughed. "I can't compete in that."

"I bet you can. A couple of longer runs, and I think you would be good to go."

Wes shook his head in disbelief as he watched the kids play. After a long pause, he asked, "You think so, huh?"

"I do."

"Well, okay, I guess," Wes said softly. "But I think you're trying to kill me."

Roxie could only giggle in response.

CHAPTER 21

KIAWAH

The half had come and gone on a glorious, cool morning. It was the kind of fall day you dream about in the upstate of South Carolina.

The kids got to cheer for Wes in his first half-marathon. Roxie took the kids on the fun run and got ice cream while Wes ran. The zoo was wonderful, and the kids really enjoyed it. The trip went just as Roxie had hoped, and everyone had a fun day.

About a week after the trip, Joan summoned Wes to her office.

When he got to her doorway, Roxie was sitting in one chair. Joan motioned for Wes to take a seat in the other one.

"Am I in trouble?" Wes asked.

"No, but we might be," Joan said as she smiled at Roxie. "We have been talking, and we would like to give you a special Christmas present if you will accept it. We all appreciate everything you've done here. The kids love you, and I really like how you have gotten them interested in running."

"Thanks," Wes said. *What is this leading to?*

"One of our volunteers has a house at Kiawah Island down near Charleston that she lets us use once in a while. She has offered it to us the second weekend in December. I was hoping you and Roxie would come with us to help watch the kids. I don't know who all we might have here then, but I'm sure some of them have never seen the ocean. I was thinking it would be a good time of the year to take them down there. Would you like to go?"

"Are you kidding? Sure," Wes said. "It's been a long time since I've seen the ocean too."

"Good," Joan said. "I was hoping you would say that." She glanced at Roxie. "There is one other thing."

"What?" Wes asked.

"Roxie tells me they have a marathon on Kiawah Island on the second weekend in December. Would you be interested in running in it?"

"No way," Wes said. "Those guys are crazy. I'm no marathoner. That half was good enough for me."

Roxie said, "Wes, you've won everything you tried this summer. You smoked 'em at that half in Greenville, and I'm sure there were some good runners there too. I'm sure the kids would love it. Besides, we have already taken up the money for the entry fee."

"Wes, you do whatever you want," Joan said. "We just thought it might be a good opportunity. Free place to stay—and the kids really get excited when they see you do well."

"At least think about it?" Roxie said. "It is flat after all."

"You are crazy." Wes laughed and looked at Roxie. "But I'll think about it."

A marathon, Wes thought in the days after their conversation, *is suicidal.* He had raced 3.1 miles, 6.2 miles, and now 13.1 miles, but 26.2 miles was unimaginable. He knew what it was like to go out hard in the shorter distances, maintain a fast pace, and leave something for the final sprint. But the psychology behind the marathon was totally different. It was less aerobic than the shorter distances and more of a mental battle. He had heard that the mind instinctively tells you to slow down before the body shuts down as a survival move. It's a major struggle to keep the body moving when the muscles are screaming for rest, but the thought piqued his interest. *Maybe it would be a good time to take advantage of the opportunity. Do one just to see what it is like—and then check it off the list.* Those were the thoughts racing around in his mind as he went out on a longer sixteen-mile run that weekend to sort it out.

In the meantime, Roxie was going on the offensive. All of the employees and volunteers at the home began to congratulate Wes on entering and wished him luck. Of course, the kids were talking about it and hoping they would still be there. The icing on the cake was little blonde-headed, blue-eyed four-year-old Allie. "Roxie says if I'm here long enough, I get to go to the beach and watch you win a race."

Wes could only shake his head and laugh.

After a week of internal debate, Wes said, "Okay, Roxie. You win. I'll give it a try. That was a nice touch with Allie, but I want to know why you are pushing me."

"All right! That's great." She pumped her fist. "Why? I see a lot of potential. I really believe in Romans 8:28, and I think God has big plans for you. I don't know how or why, but he has blessed you with a lot of talent. I'm curious to see how He can use it for His glory. Does that make sense?"

"Okay, Preacher. I've heard that before. I like Romans 8:28 too. I guess we'll see what happens."

"Preacher?" Roxie asked.

Wes laughed. "It's a long story. I'll tell you sometime."

Wes dove into his training. He read everything he could about marathon training and developed a training regimen. It was definitely different from the training he had done in the past. Varying distances each day—increasing and decreasing miles— he gradually acclimated his body to the longer distance and threw in speed work once a week to keep his pace up. His long runs on the weekends were anywhere from twelve to twenty-three miles. He was able to run with Tim and the Lander cross-country team. Their coach, Joe Hopkins, was a good source of marathon training information. It was definitely a challenge, but he felt up to the task. As a general rule, shorter-distance guys did better when they stepped up to the marathon than longer distance guys did when they ran shorter races. It was easier to gain endurance than it was to gain speed. Wes was hoping that would be the case for him.

He had class on Mondays, Wednesdays, and Fridays at ten thirty. He was able to run early, go to class, and then go to the store and the home in the evening. On Saturdays, he did his long runs and made the trip to the McMarriott to see his friends. On Sunday mornings, Wes went to worship services at First Baptist Church with Roxie. On Sunday evenings, they went to Anthony's Bible study. It was a busy life, but he was on a mission. He was so thankful that God had reached down and saved him and placed him at the Bowers-Rodgers Home. Wes just wanted to do the best he could for Him to reach the kids and set a good example for others.

When December rolled around, the race was just two weeks away. That was the hardest time for a marathoner, especially a first-timer. The hard training is over, the long runs are done, and it's time to taper. It's been said that you can't win a marathon in the two weeks before a marathon, but you can sure lose one. You feel guilty for not running more as if you had not done enough, but that is the time to cut back on the miles, rest more, and fuel up for the race. If you continue to run harder and not get enough rest, you will pay the price on race day with a tired, subpar performance. It's hard to sleep. The body is not as tired, and the mind is racing. The ponies want out of the stable to go for a run, but it's time for restraint.

That was truly the case for Wes. Time crept along, and he wondered if race day would ever arrive. He had finished his class for the semester. There were eight nice, well-behaved kids at the home, and things were pretty quiet. He and Roxie had taken them running at the civic center and given them their T-shirts. They were getting excited about the race too. Allie was still there, and it looked like she was going to get to see the ocean after all.

On the day before the race, they packed the van with their eight young kids. Wes and Roxie shared the driving, and Joan and her husband followed in their car.

Roxie said, "Since I got you into this, I'll do the majority of the driving. Besides you need to be carbo-loading, don't you?" Carbo-loading was something Wes was not accustomed to with shorter distances since endurance was not as big an issue. The human body generally had enough energy stored up to run twenty miles, but it was essential for marathoners to eat extra carbohydrates in the forty-eight hours before a race. This ensures that they have enough gas in the tank to go 26.2 miles without fading or *bonking* as it's called in running parlance. Wes had made his own trail mix with nuts, raisins, granola, and a little dark chocolate to go with the extra potatoes and pasta he had been eating.

They arrived at the condo after an uneventful three-hour drive, and the kids shot out of the van like cannonballs. All they could talk about was the beach, and the excitement was killing them. They unloaded quickly, and Wes and Roxie decided to take the kids to the beach for a while—as if they had a choice in the matter. The water was too cold for a swim, but the kids could not resist running in and out of the shallow tide in their bare feet. The temperature was almost seventy degrees with no clouds or wind, but it felt even warmer than that.

Wes stared at the ocean, lost in his thoughts.

Allie came up with Roxie and said, "What are you doing, Wes?"

"Oh, just thinking. I was trying to remember the last time I'd been to the beach. It's been a long, long time." He gave Roxie a quick smile and said, "Come on, little sister. Let's go find some seashells." They gathered seashells, a few crab shells, and even a small horseshoe crab shell for souvenirs. They couldn't have asked for a better winter day on the South Carolina coast. A very good time was had by all.

Afterward, Wes and Roxie drove down to the office at the East Beach area with the kids, so Wes could check in for the race. He got his bib and his white entrant's long-sleeved running shirt with the design of a stork walking in the ocean reeds. *Guess I'm official now.* There was a small pond behind the office with a nice wooden deck where they had set up little fires in pots and were giving out cookies and cocoa. They all got a treat and looked out over the pond for alligators, which were rumored to be in the area.

After a little while, Roxie said, "Who's ready for some spaghetti besides me and Wes? He needs to eat and get to bed early. Tomorrow's a big day."

Back at the condo, Joan and Al had already started preparing the spaghetti feast. After the big meal, they all watched a Disney movie and were in bed by nine.

Wes had a fitful night of tossing and turning, which was to be expected the night before any marathon, but it was even worse before the first marathon. He had read that it was more important to sleep well two nights before a marathon than the night before. He sure hoped that was true as he rolled out of bed at six and onto his knees for his morning prayers. He hurriedly ate a bagel, a banana, and some oatmeal.

Roxie would go with Wes to the start, and Joan and Al would bring the kids later.

"You ready?" Roxie asked as they rode the shuttle to the start line.

"I'd feel a lot better if I were watching you run 26.2 miles instead of the other way around," Wes replied.

"At least you still have your sense of humor. Isn't that a sign of being well prepared?"

"Or brain damage," Wes smirked.

The weather was perfect for a marathon—no wind, dry, and temperatures around forty degrees. The race started at eight o'clock on the cobblestone driveway lined with palm trees in front of the office where they had checked in the day before. After a short warm-up, Wes moved to the start line to get a spot at the front. The starting area was narrow, and he definitely didn't want to get bogged down in traffic.

This is crazy, he thought as he looked skyward. *I don't know what your plan is, Lord, but I hope somehow I can bring glory to You this day. And if it's okay with You, let me live through this.*

The gun soon went off, and Wes was running his first and last marathon as far as he was concerned. Since the Kiawah Island half-marathon and full marathon started at the same time, it was going to be hard to know which race the people in front of him were doing. But since it was two laps for the full, it would thin out soon enough. Wes knew that it was one race where he was going to have to watch his pace and not take off too fast because that could hurt him in the end. He tried to settle in to a comfortable pace and let the jackrabbits go.

After several hundred yards, they made the turn onto Governor's Drive, the main road on the island, and Wes tried to take in the scenery. The palm trees were beautiful, massive oak branches extended over the road, and Spanish moss hung like a veil. It was beautiful and a little spooky in the cool early morning light with the runners' breath rising like a fog over the throng.

After the first mile, they ran by some of the huge residential homes on the island. They were all very tastefully decorated for

Christmas and looked straight out of *Southern Living* magazine. The runners had thinned somewhat, the road was smooth, and he was enjoying the views. *I bet you won't see any tacky decorations in this neck of the woods.* At the two-mile marker, Wes glanced at his running watch and saw he was at twelve minutes or six minutes per mile. *Right on target. Breathing feels good. Let's just stay right there.*

People began to drop off their paces, and with all the twists and turns of the road, it was hard to tell how many were ahead of him. Wes wore a band on his arm that gave him his target time at each mile so he could continue to try to churn out six-minute miles. It was a strange feeling for a 5K runner since his pace was slower. His breathing was not as labored, and he was not in oxygen debt. He just didn't feel like he was working as hard as he should be, but he knew it was coming. He had read that the marathon was a twenty-mile warm up and then a six-mile race. *We'll find out soon enough*, he thought as they passed the five-mile marker.

Wes knew there would be a turnaround at 6.5 miles, and he might be able to get an idea how many people were ahead of him. He would be able to see their bib colors to see if they were running the full or the half. He glanced down at his red bib to remind himself that red was full.

He was running in the street, but a runner came toward him on the bike path that bordered the road. He—and the next several runners—wore blue bibs. Wes approached a water station on the side of the road that gave runners in both directions access. Wes grabbed a cup of water from the young volunteer and took several quick sips on the run. In the process, several runners went by on the bike path, and he couldn't see their bibs. Immediately after the water station, a pole on the side of the road directed the runners to turn onto the bike path.

Wes made the 360-degree turn and thought that he was one-fourth of the way through. *That came pretty quick and wasn't too bad*, he thought. The bike path was not as smooth as the road, and he had to watch his step, but he couldn't help looking at the sea of runners still coming down the road. It seemed to go on forever.

About halfway back to the starting line, he heard drums and passed a conga band on the side of the road. *Never seen that at a cross-country meet.* He laughed and appreciated their energizing beat. He maintained his pace, and he was only passed by two sprinting college-age gazelles with blue bibs near the twelve-mile mark. Before he knew it, he could hear an announcer on the speakers at the finish.

There were more spectators along the side of the bike path, and he knew he was almost halfway home. Sure enough, Wes soon came to a volunteer holding a sign at a fork in the path: Halfers to the left and the finish line. Full to the right and more fun. It was cruel to watch the folks ahead turn to the left and rest. He turned to the right to start his second lap.

From the side of the road, Roxie yelled, "You're fifth, Wes. Keep it up. Looking good."

"*Huh? Four ahead of me? Better than I thought.* He gave her the thumbs-up sign and kept going. He took stock of how he felt: breathing was still good, legs felt good, not tired yet. He felt like he had something left and kept plugging along at his pace. He saw one runner about thirty yards ahead and thought he would try to gradually catch him. But no hurry. Not yet anyway.

The emerging sun was burning off the morning dew, but the temperature was still cool. There were water stations every two miles, so Wes got a sip of water on the run every time. He didn't feel thirsty, but he knew that once he did, it would be too late. He wouldn't be able to replace it fast enough, and his pace would suffer. At the sixteen-mile water station, he caught and passed the runner ahead of him. *Three runners to go, but none in sight. Just don't get passed.* He wanted to finish strong and not give up any spots at the end.

As he approached the turnaround again, Wes saw the first runner. With his long legs striding easily and his face relaxed, he looked strong, like he had done it a lot. About one-fourth of a mile separated them. It wasn't long before he saw the other two runners coming toward him on the bike path, and Wes had not made the turn yet. He passed the water station, and to make matters worse, the turnaround pole had been moved back about thirty yards. That meant he had more distance to make up than he thought. *I don't think I'm catching them*, he thought. He knew how important it was to stay positive. *Just keep working. They may fall off their pace.*

He made the turn, grabbed more water, and decided it was time to pick up his pace a little. Another mile clicked by, and he saw the next runner make the turn onto Flyway Drive. Wes continued to press and soon was on the guy's heels.

Wes gambled when he saw the guy reach for water at mile 21. Not slowing at all for water, Wes picked up his pace and was quickly ten yards ahead of the other runner. He glanced at his pace chart and realized he had lowered his pace to 5:50 per mile. *Five miles to go—and two runners to catch. Too early to go all out.* He decided to try to stay around 5:50 pace and hope the two ahead of him were slowing. He was beginning to feel the strain in his legs, and he noticed he was breathing harder.

Wes was now entering what's known as the Zombie Zone—the twilight zone past mile 20. Weird things can start happening to competitive runners in this no-man's-land. That was where training and preparation started to show their true colors. *Did I do enough long runs or not enough? Did I get enough rest or taper too early? Did I eat enough carbs?* And then there was the mental aspect. The body is weary, but the mind is wearier. You feel like there is more lactic acid in your veins than blood and oxygen carrying hemoglobin. Runners have been known to slip over into la-la land, thinking the race is over, and sitting down in the road, and taking their shoes off with several miles left to go. *It's such a puzzle. All the pieces that have to come together to have a good race.*

Wes had heard the stories, and he knew that was where the mental battle intensified. You feel like you are running as hard as you can, but your pace begins to slow with every mile. The legs have had enough of the beating, the calves feel like they could knot up in cramps at any second, and the body is screaming for stillness and rest. Up to that point, it hasn't been as much of an aerobic workout like a 5K or 10K, but as the lactic acid level goes up and the oxygen debt rises correspondingly, it becomes a struggle to get enough oxygen. That was where Wes soon found himself. Some runners try mental tricks to will their bodies over their minds. They sing to themselves, count, think of things that start with each letter of the alphabet—anything to keep moving and not think about the pain.

For Wes, he had several wells to dip into for motivation. First of all, he prayed. He thanked God for the beautiful day and the opportunity to be out there. As always, he thanked Him for his second chance and his desire to bring glory to Him. He asked for the strength to finish strong and set a good example for the kids. He repeated the twenty-third psalm. Second, Wes thought of Preacher and his command to run for him. He thought of his friends in the prison. *What a story this will be for them.* Lastly, as fatigue really started to set in, he thought of his father and the crows and their negative chatter. The last thought only stayed briefly. Wes knew that he had found new meaning in life, and that thought was only one of the schemes of Satan to challenge his witness.

Another two miles slipped by, and Wes decided it was now-or-never time. He was tired, in a lot of pain, and had no experience in the marathon, but he was determined to finish strong. They were back on the curving road now, and he decided to push the pace. He couldn't see anyone ahead of him, but the few spectators he saw encouraged him to go. As he approached the water station at mile 24, he wasn't sure if he was hallucinating or if it was just a spectator, but he thought he saw another runner in the distance. Mirage or not, he took a quick sip of water on the run and pressed ahead.

The course turned back onto a bike path, and sure enough, there was a runner just ahead. Wes was trying to decide if he should hang back and try to take him at the finish or press on. *Wish I knew how far ahead the next guy is*, he thought. *And how he's doing.* After a short internal debate, he decided he had enough left in the tank to press on—and he sure didn't want to take a chance on anyone catching him from behind.

It wasn't long till he had caught and passed this next rabbit as they reached the mile 25 sign. *Only 1.2 miles to go,* he thought. *Press on. Keep pushing. We're almost there.* He flew through the last water station with no sign of the next runner ahead of him. With less than a mile to go, the nice, flat course threw in a surprise—a small twenty-foot hill. Normally, it would mean nothing, but to a body that has just covered 25.5 miles for the first time at a very fast pace and was trying to catch some unknown sprinter ahead, it was slightly demoralizing. *You've got to be kidding,* he thought as he willed his body over it as quickly as he could. *Just don't fall down now.*

Wes could hear the announcer in the distance, and since he hadn't announced a winner, the competition was still out there. He came to the point where the halfers got to take it home, and it was his turn—one-tenth of a mile to go. He slipped back into the wide street as he made the left turn for home. Portable fencing kept the fans out of the road. One more turn—and he would be there. Still no announcement of a winner. Suddenly, he heard his name.

Roxie and the kids were screaming, "Go! Go! Go!"

Wes quickly pointed to his Warrior shirt, which he had decided to wear to surprise them, and returned his attention to the task at hand.

Wes made the last turn, and forty yards ahead of him, he saw the winner breaking the tape at the finish line. *So close, so close,* he thought. He wanted to crumble in the road, but he sprinted in, touching his hand to his heart and pointing skyward in acknowledgement and gratitude to God for seeing him through. Wes crossed the line in second place in his first marathon. He bent over, hands on his knees, gasping for breath. Race officials grabbed his arms to steady him and make sure he was okay as he froze in place for a few seconds. Straightening up and nodding that he was okay, he congratulated the winner and slowly moved on through the finish area.

His gang was waiting. "Wes, Wes, you did it. You did it," they screamed. "And you wore our shirt."

"You bet I did. Thanks for coming, Warriors." Turning his gaze to Roxie, he frowned and said, "I'm sorry. I couldn't quite catch him."

"Sorry. Sorry for what? You finished second at your first marathon. That's amazing."

"I know, but I wanted to win for the kids."

"Wes, as far as these kids are concerned, you did win. You were great. And do you have any idea who that guy who won is?" Roxie asked. "I heard some officials talking about him at the start. That's Kenny Newby. He is going to the Olympic trials next year and is considered one of the five best in the country. Can you believe it? In your first marathon, you almost caught him. Wow!".

"Really? That's interesting," Wes replied as his exhausted mind tried to process the information.

Joan, Al, and Allie caught up with them. The little one waved and said, "Hey, Wes. Can we go to the beach now?"

They all had a good laugh.

Wes took a sip of water and said, "Sure. If I can keep up."

At that point, a middle-aged man caught up with them. "Excuse me. I just wanted to thank you for your witness. I like your shirt, and I saw what you did at the finish." The man pointed skyward.

"Thank you," Wes replied. "It's all for Him."

CHAPTER 22

MENDED FENCES

The rest of the trip went wonderfully. The kids had a great time frolicking on the beach Saturday afternoon. The weather was beautiful.

Understandably, Wes was not moving very fast. His felt really tired, but he was just thankful for the experience. He was able to get a free massage at the finish before they went to the beach, and that had helped tremendously.

On Sunday morning, the kids and adults all slept late, and after a satisfying brunch, they decided to go for one more walk on the beach before heading home. The kids were worn out from all the fun, and they slept most of the way back—as did Wes. It was almost seven o'clock when the van pulled into the Bowers-Rodgers parking lot.

"That was a great trip. Thank you, guys, for going," Joan said as Wes and Roxie unloaded the kids from the van.

One of the weekend mothers came out and asked to speak to Joan alone. Wes and Roxie glanced at each other, wondering what had happened.

After a short conversation, Joan called for Wes to come over and speak to her alone.

Joan said, "Wes, there was a call from Walhalla this morning. Your father has cancer and is at the hospice house there. He's asking to see you."

Wes stared at Joan for a few seconds. With Preacher's help, he had long ago come to terms with his relationship with his father. His Heavenly Father loved him no matter what. Wes knew he couldn't change the past. He had been determined to focus on taking each day one at a time and making the best decisions he could one by one. He wouldn't let the scars of the past cloud his future any longer, but he'd known this day was coming. He had wondered how it would go down. Would he see his father again or would there be no contact? And if there were contact, how would it be? Would it be one last bitter stab from his father—or would he try to make amends?

Wes had always hoped there would be contact. After all that happened, it was weird that he still hoped it might somehow work out. *Could it end on a good note? Every son needs a father and longs for that relationship. You always hope they will change.*

Joan touched Wes softly on the arm. "Wes, would you like us to go with you? We will be glad to drive you."

Regaining his focus, Wes said, "No. This is something I need to do myself. Thanks anyway."

"Okay, I understand. Take all the time you need," Joan replied.

The drive to Walhalla took one hour and thirty minutes through the back roads of the upstate. Wes gathered his thoughts and played through different scenarios. What would he say if his father was mean and ugly? He had determined he would not retaliate in kind. That was not who he was now, and he didn't want it to end that way. What if he was apologetic? Wes prayed for the strength to handle himself in a Christian way so things would end on a positive note.

Arriving at the hospice house, he soon found himself outside his father's room. He took a deep breath and slowly pushed the door open. Wes was not prepared for what he saw. His father was alone and sleeping. Gone was the healthy, strong man with the thick head of wavy, greased-back black hair that Wes had feared for so long. In his place was a frail, old, weak, white-haired shell of a man.

Wes was immediately filled with compassion for his father and what the disease had done to him. *That man is no longer someone to be scared of.*

Wes moved to the side of the bed and waited. After a few minutes, his father stirred and opened his eyes a little. He closed them and slowly licked his lips.

Wes said, "Hey."

To his surprise, his father raised his right hand slowly and reached for Wes.

Wes took his hand, and his father held on to Wes's hand and did not let go. Wes asked, "How you doing?"

In a weak, raspy voice, his father said, "Pretty rough." He pointed for Wes to come around to the other side of the bed. Wes moved to the other side of the bed, took a seat, and moved the chair closer to the bed.

His father raised his left hand to grasp Wes's hand and did not let go.

"How's life been treating you?" his father asked.

"Oh, up and down, I guess." Wes looked for signs of where things were going.

"I'm sorry it's been up and down for you," his father slowly replied.

Wes searched for the right words. "Are they treating you okay here?"

"Yeah, pretty good." After a pause, he added, "I guess they've put me here to die."

A nurse came in and asked if he needed anything.

Wes's father replied, "My son is here. He will take care of me."

Wes was taken aback at his sudden stature as chosen caregiver. *This is interesting, but better than I expected.*

When his father closed his eyes and nodded off, Wes glanced at the nurse.

She said, "He'll do that a lot. Sometimes they nod off in mid-sentence. We give them just enough pain medicine to keep them out of pain but not totally zonked out, so they are alert periodically. It's all normal."

"How long does he have?" Wes asked.

"Hard to say," she replied. "Could be today—or it could be a week. No longer, I doubt."

Wes was caught a little off guard by her candid assessment. After all, he wasn't asking when his laundry would be ready or when a package might arrive. This was someone's life they were talking about—even if it was his long-lost father. Given his father's positive response to Wes being there, he found himself tentatively hoping for a little more time.

"He's been coming and going like this for a few days. They gradually start sleeping more and having more trouble breathing. A pretty sure sign is if they start having hallucinations. But you never know. They can rebound for a while or slip away quietly and quickly."

They stared at the patient for a minute.

"Well, my name is JoAnn. I'll be here tonight. You're welcome to stay. You can sleep on the couch over there if you'd like. There are sheets and a blanket in the closet too. Call me if you need anything else."

Wes asked if there was a phone he could use, and JoAnn directed him to the nurse's station. He called Joan and told her it didn't look like it would be long and asked if he could stay a few days. She told him absolutely and said they would be praying for him. He quickly returned to his father's room.

He began a vigil of listening for his father to stir to alertness so they could share a few stolen moments. *No one wants to die alone, and that seems to be the case here.* Their conversations floated back to shared good times when they went hunting or fishing. That was when Wes had seen his father relaxed and at his best, and he didn't mind reliving those memories. No mention was made of the elephant in the room—the bad times, his mother, all the excess baggage his father had left him with. Wes was a little surprised that his father asked very little of Wes's life other than where he was working. Wes continued to keep the conversation positive to not upset his father, all the while hoping there could be some positive resolution to their relationship.

Wes thought they were on the verge of that when his father awoke with a shudder shortly after two o'clock in the morning. He generally would sleep for an hour or so and then wake up for fifteen or twenty minutes, and they would talk. Since he was still exhausted from his run, Wes was having no trouble nodding off, but he was not sleeping so soundly that he did not wake when his father stirred. Jumping up, Wes sensed his father's uneasiness, "Hey, I'm here," he said.

His father blinked several times and said, "Good. Sit down over here." He pointed to a chair on the other side of his bed. "I want to tell you something."

Wes took a deep breath and wondered if it was the moment of reckoning.

His father said, "I saw several people in the corner over there just now." He pointed to an empty chair on the other side of the room.

Wes exhaled, realizing it wasn't the talk he had hoped for. "Did it scare you?" he asked.

"Scared the daylights out of me," his father said, almost chuckling.

He blinked and drifted off to sleep before Wes could ask if it was anyone he recognized.

Why couldn't it have been different? Why couldn't his touch have been something to look forward to instead of fearing? He couldn't help but find it ironic that with every waking second his father wanted Wes to hold his hand. *Is he being his usual selfish self and is afraid of dying alone? Or is he trying to make amends and reach out in a final gesture of love in the only way he knows how?* Grasping for positive closure, Wes accepted it as his father's effort at peace.

Wes drifted back to sleep and slept until almost eight thirty. Seeing daylight coming through the curtains and realizing he had been sleeping over six hours, he jumped.

Wes's father was still breathing.

Wes breathed a sigh of relief and wondered what it meant that they had been asleep so long.

A new nurse stuck her head in and asked, "Still sleeping, huh?" As Wes nodded, she added, "Sometimes they'll sleep like that all day."

"What does it mean?"

"Hard to say," this new nurse said. "Holler if you need us. My name is Stacie."

At lunchtime, his father was still sleeping soundly. Wes stayed in the room all afternoon, hoping it was not the end. He had things he still wanted to say and things he hoped to hear. It was weighing heavily on his mind when his father stirred around four. He sleepily asked for a sip of water and then drifted back.

This isn't looking good, Wes thought.

The doctor came by and asked Wes how it was going. Listening to his patient's breathing, he told Wes it might not be much longer.

At nine, Wes was washing his hands in the bathroom when he heard his father stirring. He rushed over to his father's side, grasped his hand, and said, "Hey. I'm here. It's okay."

His father blinked several times and stared at the ceiling.

Wes knew he had to seize the moment. "I just wanted to say I'm sorry for the way things worked out between us. I forgive you—and I hope you forgive me."

His father blinked several times as if fighting to stay conscious. "I forgive you." He swallowed hard and repeated slowly, "I forgive you. I forgive you." His voice was soft and quiet as sleep again took over.

For several minutes, Wes blinked back tears. His mind flashed back to when his pet parakeet died when he was six years old. Wes had a proper burial for it in the backyard and even took a Bible outside to read a few verses. As he had stood there, Bible in hand and tears on his cheeks, his father came up and mockingly said, "Are you going to cry when I die?" He chuckled and walked off.

Wes had replayed that memory over the years and wondered what the outcome would be. He knew he was watching his father slip away. The tears began to flow quietly and slowly. Even though he made peace with the situation long ago, he finally felt his burden being lifted. He didn't get his apology, but they both got something infinitely better: peace. If those were to be the last words exchanged between them, Wes knew they would both be able to rest in peace. The fence had been mended.

Wes sat down beside the bed and continued to hold his father's hand as he prayed. He asked God to forgive his father for his sins and to please take good care of him. He also asked for forgiveness for not honoring his father as he should have regardless of his behavior. Lastly, he thanked God for allowing him to be there with him and for allowing them to end on a good note.

His father did not wake up again. JoAnn woke Wes at five and told him it wouldn't be long.

His father's breathing was labored. Within thirty minutes, he took several deep breaths and passed on with his son holding his hand. Wes couldn't help but notice how peaceful he looked.

JoAnn gave Wes a hug and told him he could stay with him until the funeral home arrived. It was about thirty minutes before they arrived and took the body. Wes found out from the hospice office that his father had worked out his funeral arrangements in advance with instructions to be buried by Grandma Strong the day after he passed. With the plans in place, Wes decided to return to Greenwood to get some rest and some clothes for the funeral.

When he pulled in his driveway in Greenwood, Roxie was sitting in the porch swing on his front porch.

He said, "What are you doing here? It's freezing out here."

"I called the hospice house this morning to check on you, and they said you had already left. Wes, I'm so sorry." She gave him a quick hug.

"Thanks. I hadn't seen him in a long time. You want to come in?"

"Sure," she answered.

They sat on Wes's couch, and he said, "I'm not sure how much you know about my parents—"

Without letting him finish, she said, "I knew you didn't have anyone. I thought they were dead."

"No, my mom died in a car wreck, but I hadn't seen my father since he kicked her out before the wreck while I was at Clemson.

He was pretty abusive, mostly verbal, and when he kicked her out, I told her she did not have to live like that any longer. So she was making it on her own, and he blamed me for the breakup. I never saw him again until now. He was always pretty rough on us, and I wasn't sure how this was going to go. I had made peace with it and finally realized when I was saved that the past was over. I couldn't change any of it, but there was still a lot of baggage from my childhood. It's always been there in the shadows—whether I wanted to admit it or not. I guess it ended as well as it could have."

Roxie listened intently while Wes told her about his last conversations with his father.

When Wes finished, she said, "I don't understand. What did you have to apologize for?"

"It wasn't about me. He was a frail, pitiful old man on his deathbed. In his way of looking at things, I had caused him harm. One of us had to make it right, and if it took me apologizing to him to allow him to die in peace, then I needed to do it. To have our last words to each other be that we forgave each other, I think there was a lot of healing in that for the both of us." Wes placed his face in his hands to hide his tears.

Roxie slid closer, put her left arm around Wes, and rested her right hand on his knee. She rested her head on his shoulder. Through his tears, he said, "Look, Roxie. I don't know what you know about me, but I've made a lot of mistakes. I'm not—"

"What? Not perfect? Neither am I," she said. "Wes, I know what happened—about prison, your addiction. Joan felt like I should know since we would be working closely together. I also know you're not who you were. God is working a miracle in you. I see how you touch our kids with your Bible stories. You've got a gift for reaching them—and also for running. I don't know God's plan, but I know He is going to work it all out for good. Do you understand?"

Wes nodded slowly.

With her right hand, Roxie touched his chin and turned his head to look her in the eyes. "Do you understand, Wes Strong? God loves you—and I think I do too." She softly kissed his cheek.

CHAPTER 23

MERRY CHRISTMAS

The graveside funeral was conducted the next morning at eleven by the chaplain at the hospice house. *How sad to not have a personal relationship with a pastor to deliver your eulogy,* Wes thought.

The chaplain did a nice job. Wes regretted that he had not taken the opportunity to talk to his father about God, but he knew he had liked to watch Billy Graham on TV. He felt like his father had believed, and he hoped his father had developed a closer relationship with God over the years.

Joan and Roxie were there. Wes saw some of his old neighbors and some of his distant cousins. He felt relieved and thankful that he and his father had ended on a good note. He felt like that chapter of his life was finally past. He could finally move on.

Wes went back at work early the next day and tapped timidly on Joan's door.

"Come in," she said. "You didn't have to come today."

"I know, and I appreciate it," Wes said. "But you guys are really the only family I've got. I just wanted to be here."

"I understand," Joan replied. "I know it was hard. If there is anything we can do, just let us know."

"You already have. You have been so good to me, and I am so appreciative. I definitely don't want to do anything to jeopardize my job here. I really like it, and I think we are helping these kids—"

Joan said, "What are you getting at, Wes?"

"Well," Wes said.

"Spit it out," Joan said.

"Okay, um, I wanted to ask your permission to maybe ask Roxie out." Wes held his breath.

"Like on a date?" Joan teased. "I don't know."

"If you don't want me to, I understand—but I promise to not let it interfere with my job."

"Relax," Joan said with a laugh. "Of course you can. I think it's a wonderful idea. You two make a nice couple, and I know you will keep it discreet in front of the children."

"Oh, yes, ma'am. Yes, ma'am," Wes said. "Thank you."

Wes's feet barely touched the ground as he headed out to the playground.

When Roxie and the kids saw him coming, they all ran and gave him hugs. Then, they asked if they could play soccer. "Sounds good to me. I could use a game," Wes said with a big smile. Roxie looked at him curiously, wondering what was up.

After they had tucked the kids into bed, they straightened up the toddler's playroom on the first floor while the night-shift ladies put clothes in the washer in the basement. Wes nervously made small talk as they picked up the toys scattered about the room.

Wes finally sat down and watched Roxie for a minute.

She looked at him with a grin and said, "What's up? You've been acting kind of weird today."

Wes smiled and wrung his hands nervously. "Well, I was wondering if maybe Saturday night, if you weren't doing anything, that maybe I could take you out to eat and maybe to a movie?"

"Why, Wes Strong, are you asking me out?" Roxie teased.

Wes nodded and said, "I asked Joan, and she said it's okay!"

Roxie laughed. "Well, I've heard of asking the father's permission, but I've never heard of asking the boss's permission." Sticking her hand out to shake Wes's hand, she said, "I accept your proposal, sir."

Two weeks later, when Wes and Roxie arrived at the Bowers-Rodgers Home employee Christmas party, Susan met them at the door. "You two are perfect for each other! And what are you doing trying to hide it from me? I'm so happy for you!"

"Thank you," they replied at the same time.

Two days before Christmas, there were only three children at the home. Volunteers had agreed to take the kids out for the evening so the employees could have some time together. It was a festive occasion with lots of food, music, and laughter. The home generally was inundated with decorations, food, sweets, and gifts for the kids from churches and well-wishers during the holiday season. The employees each brought a dish for a meal, and there was definitely a feast.

Not being much of a cook, Wes helped Roxie make a tossed salad. Wes was feeling especially thankful to be experiencing his first Christmas with freedom in a long time. And having Roxie in his life especially lifted his spirits. Having already received the best presents he could ask for, it would definitely be the best Christmas ever.

After the meal, they exchanged gifts. Wes had drawn Susan's name and gave her a scented candle that Roxie had helped him pick out. It was a merry time with lots of laughter. As time went on, Wes's name was not called, but he didn't notice. He was having a wonderful time watching everybody else open gifts.

When they were all done, Joan said, "Is that everybody?"

All eyes turned to Wes.

Joan said, "Oh, yes, Mr. Wes. Roxie, would you like to do the honors?"

"I sure would." She jumped up from her seat beside Wes.

Wes furrowed his brow, wondering what was up.

Roxie cleared her throat and said, "Wes, we all have been amazed at the job you've done with the kids. They love you, and we love you. Me most of all," she added under her breath.

Everyone cracked up.

"We're one big family here, and we are so happy you are part of our family now. We know God has big plans for you here. We also know he has big plans for you as a runner. *So*, we have all pitched in and are sending you to the Boston Marathon in April!"

Everyone clapped and cheered.

Wes's mouth dropped open. "No, no." He waved his hand and shook his head. "That's got to be way too expensive. I can't let you guys do that."

Joan said, "We worked it all out, Wes, with actually very little expense. One of the volunteers has a brother who is a pilot with Delta, and he can fly you to Boston for fifty dollars round-trip under his family benefits plan. And I know several people who have reward points for staying at Holiday Inns. I got them to donate some points and got you four nights at a Holiday Inn Express in Cambridge, which is just outside of Boston. That only left the entry fee, and we took care of that. Roxie is right. You have meant a lot to us already, and we wanted to just say thank you. Now say yes and go make us proud."

"Y'all, I don't know what to say," Wes stammered.

"Say yes!" they all said loudly.

"Okay, okay." Wes looked at Roxie. "Wow! Me in the Boston Marathon? I never would have imagined. Thank you. Thank you so much!"

When Roxie sat back down beside Wes, he touched her softly on the hand. "Was this your idea?"

"Well?" she giggled.

"Well, thank you." Wes smiled. "This is really special. This is the best Christmas ever!"

"I knew you qualified at Kiawah, and I knew you would never think of going on your own. Besides, you are running really strong, and I think something special might happen. Like I have been saying, God has big plans for you."

"You always say that," Wes said with a smile.

"And I haven't been wrong yet, have I?" she said with a laugh.

"Guess I better get running then," Wes said. "I've read it's a tough, hilly course."

Roxie said, "Hills shouldn't be a challenge for a cross-country runner like you. Who knows? They may even help you." She smiled and patted him on the back.

Wes nodded. How could he have ever imagined a year ago where he would be now? He was so grateful and happy. What a merry Christmas!

With Boston only four months away, Wes threw himself into this new challenge with a solid determination to make everyone proud. He was not an elite runner, but that did not stop him from wanting to prepare as best he could without taking away from his job, school, and other responsibilities. The Boston Marathon is the greatest all-star running event in the world. Elite runners are invited based on their current status in the running world. Amateurs gain acceptance if they meet the qualifying time for their age group at a Boston Marathon-certified marathon. Elite runners start with the amateurs directly behind them. No other sporting event in the world pits the pros and the amateurs on the same playing field at the same time.

To qualify and be included in this great sports extravaganza is the pinnacle of any distance runner's career. The qualifying times are stringent, so that only the best of the best are allowed to participate. Many people spend a lot of time, effort, and money striving to reach this goal. For most runners, it is an impossible dream. For some, it is possible with enough training and the proper alignment of the stars at a fast, flat, qualifying marathon. For a lucky few, it is regularly achieved without requiring superhuman effort. Wes Strong fell into this latter group. He knew he had qualified at Kiawah—at his first marathon—but actually going had not crossed his mind. Now that he was going, he was determined to make the most of it.

He got back in touch with Joe Hopkins, the Lander cross-country coach, for advice. It just so happened that Joe had run Boston a couple times, and he was an invaluable source of guidance for Wes as he prepared. Wes was trying to read as much information as he could about the course and how to train, but having Joe around to verify the information was a great help. He learned that Boston would be quite different than Kiawah. Even though Boston has lots of hills, it actually ends up at a negative altitude gain. In other words, even though the runners climb a lot of hills, overall they go downhill more.

Joe helped Wes devise a training program that included lots of hill training and focused on the downhill aspect as much as the uphill portion. Having actually run Boston, Joe was able to explain to Wes that runners had to be careful in the first half of the race not to go out too fast on the abundance of early downhills. The downhill pounding on the quads would zap the legs of the energy that would be needed for the tough uphills in the latter stages of the race. That was the kind of expert advice that only comes with actual experience.

Wes added more distance to his regimen to build a strong base. He decided that it would have helped him at Kiawah since his body was still adjusting to distance running. Probably one of the most important things Joe added was weekly tempo runs with Tim and some of the other Lander runners. Those time trials of varying distances helped build up his speed at longer distances. He had to smile every time Joe mentioned a time trial since he recalled explaining time trials to Preacher and the other Freaks. If Preacher only knew how true his words had been. *Life is truly a time trial if we trust God that He is working all things for our good."*

The four months between Christmas and Boston were a blur of training, class, and work. He also had his daily shift at the home and his weekend visits to his friends in McCormick. The best part of it all was he actually got paid to spend time with Roxie. Their love was blossoming like the spring flowers.

"Best job in the world." They laughed. "How many people get paid to spend time with their significant other?"

Not that the work was all fun and games. They continued to have a steady stream of kids coming through the home. The stories were heartbreaking—physical and sexual abuse, abandonment, broken families. Wes and Roxie both knew they were there to help the kids through a tough time and plant a seed that there was hope. Hope for a better future—and hope of a life spent growing in Christ. For the most part, they would never know if those seeds sprouted, but they both knew their job was to try. The results would be up to the Master Gardener himself.

Wes was so grateful for all the wonderful opportunities he had been given in the past year. He found himself in a continuous state of prayer, thanking God for his second chance. As Preacher said, it was not for us to understand why certain things happened, but for Wes, they all led to this place and time. He wanted desperately to be one of those seeds from the parable that landed on good soil and sprouted heavenly producing good fruit. That was his mission in life.

Wes knew donations were down at the home, and he wished he could help bring attention to the financial need. Those thoughts were constantly on his mind as he prepared for the run of his life.

CHAPTER 24

BOSTON

When the third week of April finally rolled around, it was time to leave for Boston.

Roxie volunteered for the one-hour drive to Greenville for his flight. Since the flight deal with Delta was only applicable during the week, Wes had to leave on Friday morning. Wes had never been on a plane. Along with the pre-marathon jitters, he was trying to hide his preflight anxiety.

It was nothing compared to Roxie's nerves. As they drove up Highway 25 on a cloudy spring day, she was like a mother hen sending her first child off to college.

"Do you have the directions to your hotel?"

"Did you bring your race acceptance that you will need at registration?"

"Did you get your running shoes?"

"What about a warm jacket?"

"Rox, I'll be okay," Wes finally said with a laugh. "We made a list, and I've got it all. I think I'm actually looking forward to flying for the first time. So, don't worry, okay?"

"Okay. I wish I were going with you now," she said.

"Me too," Wes said. "But definitely next time. Besides, one of us needs to stay with the kids this time."

Wes checked in, and they said their good-byes. He had firm instructions to call as soon as he got to his hotel to let her know everything had gone okay. Wes had to take whatever seat was left on the plane, which ended up being the last row by the window, which suited him just fine. He had a great view in a quiet area.

The flight was uneventful, and after a three-hour layover in Charlotte, Wes Strong landed at Logan International Airport in Boston. It may have been his first time in a big city, but he had prepared himself well. He knew to take the red line on the T, Boston's subway, which would take him out to his hotel in Cambridge. Since it was late in the afternoon, Wes grabbed a sub sandwich on his three-block walk . After calling Roxie to let her know everything was fine, he decided to turn in early and get an early start on his first full day in Boston.

After a restful nine-hour nap, Wes took the red line to the Park Street Terminal. When he exited the station, he was standing in the northwest corner of Boston Common. Its beautiful grassy area was crisscrossed with sidewalks and Japanese cherry trees that were just beginning to blossom. Surrounded on two sides by office buildings, apartments on the south side, and the gold-domed Massachusetts State Legislature on the other, Wes felt out of place. It was sensory overload with all the sights and sounds of the big city, but he immediately knew he would love this place with its modern buildings and pockets of history.

At a visitor's kiosk at the airport, Wes had picked up a brochure on the Freedom Trail walking tour that went to all the historic sites downtown. He decided to do that on Saturday, so that he could try to rest his legs on Sunday. He picked up the red line painted on the sidewalk that designated the trail outside the Park Street Terminal and headed toward the legislature building. He was surprised to see a large statue commemorating the first black Union regiment in the Civil War, which happened to be from Massachusetts. They were shown attacking Fort Johnson in Charleston Harbor. He thought it was interesting to see a statue commemorating a Union attack on a Confederate fort.

Well, this is the North, he thought.

Wes continued on the red trail and visited Bunker Hill across the bay and the wooden USS *Constitution* before coming back to the North End to visit Paul Revere's home. His favorite stop in this area was Old North Church and Copp's graveyard. He quickly fell in love with the Italian section of town with its tight streets and colorful banners celebrating their heritage. For lunch, Wes had some authentic Italian pasta at one of the abundant Old World restaurants before continuing on his excursion.

That afternoon, Wes went back downtown for the race expo. When he stopped on a corner to study his map, two middle-aged ladies asked what he was looking for. When he told them, they soon pointed him on his way.

I thought Charleston, South Carolina, was supposed to be the friendliest city in the United States, but I think these folks have them beat.

Wes had only been to a few race expos, but he was totally unprepared for what awaited him at the Hynes Convention Center. It was two convention-size rooms full of vendors. After proudly picking up his official bib and Boston Marathon shirt as an official runner, he wandered through the maze of vendors. He could not believe all the other runners there and the electricity in the air. It suddenly hit him that he would actually be running in the Boston Marathon. He thumped his chest with his right hand and pointed to the heavens, thanking God again for the experience. He went from booth to booth, looking at the samples of running gels, food, and running clothes. There were a lot of representatives from other races around the world.

Lots of neat places to visit. Maybe one day.

Adidas was the official vendor of Boston Marathon attire. They sold men's and women's running pants, short- and long-sleeved shirts, and official jackets—all with the distinctive unicorn logo of the Boston Athletic Association. All of it was in the bright yellow and royal blue colors of the BAA. Wes had decided he would allow himself one splurge: the official jacket and a T-shirt. He took his time enjoying the moment and finally decided on his purchases.

Time had gotten away from him, and the growl in his stomach told him it was suppertime. Wes headed back to Quincy Market, which he had passed through earlier on his Freedom Trail adventure. In the past, the building had been an indoor marketplace, and it housed dozens of food vendors under one roof. After much debate, he chose chicken teriyaki with stir-fry vegetables. He sat down at the eating area in the middle of the building and tried to absorb all he had seen that day. Without a doubt, it was one of the best days of his life. *And I haven't even run the marathon yet!*

After another good night's sleep, Wes decided to return to the expo. The energy was addictive, and he couldn't get enough of it. He enjoyed listening to the other runners having a good time, talking to the representatives from other marathons in far-off exotic places, and of the food freebies. He spent most of the morning there, and after a quick lunch, he decided there was one more famous landmark he had to see: Fenway Park, the oldest professional baseball stadium in the country.

After taking the subway to Kenmore Station, Wes walked the last two blocks to the stadium. It was just as grand and magnificent as he had seen on television with its old brick architecture and pennants hanging from the street posts. There was a game going on, and there were throngs of people in the area. He walked around the outside of the stadium, trying to take it all in. The banners represented so much sports history. When he got back around to the main entrance, he noticed that the ticket agents were leaving their posts. Taking a deep breath to get up his nerve, he approached a security guard at the entrance and asked if the game was about over.

"It's the top of the eighth," he replied. "You can go in now if you'd like."

"Really?" Wes asked. "Without a ticket?"

The burly guard with his thick Bostonian accent laughed and said, "Yeah, after the eighth starts, anyone can go in."

"Wow! Thanks." Wes hurried in as if his luck might suddenly change.

He could not believe his good fortune at being there at just the right time to get to see a couple of innings of pro baseball in person—at Fenway Park. He stood on the ground level at the back of the seats along first base. He stared in amazement at the Green Monster. The famous left field wall was directly across the infield. People were packed in like sardines, but he loved every second of it.

The hometown heroes were playing the Tampa Bay Rays and losing by one run. After a scoreless top of the eighth, Wes watched with all the excitement of a little kid as Big Papi, David Ortiz, hit a home run in the bottom of the eighth to tie it up. Wes thought that the only way his day could get any better was if the game went to extra innings—so he could see more of the game.

Neither team scored in the ninth. Extra innings! He had not moved from his spot and smiled as a teenager in front of him said, "Dad, these are real fans up here. Look at this place. Not a one has left, and all of them are still keeping score in their scorebooks. This is so cool!"

I couldn't have said it better, Wes thought.

After another scoreless inning, Ortiz again came through in the bottom of the eleventh inning when he drove in the winning run. The old stadium erupted in cheers as the celebration soon poured out into the narrow streets of Yawkey Way. Wes decided to take his time leaving because he didn't want the moment to be over. He wandered around a little and took in more of the stadium. He walked around to the seats above the Green Monster, but the attendant posted there would not let him walk out among those seats. At least he got to see what the view was like from out there. He ventured around for almost another hour before the attendants came through and told the stragglers it was time to go.

The last treat of the day was the prerace meal provided by the BAA at City Hall Plaza. Since it was included in his entrance fee, Wes didn't want to miss out on the pasta buffet. It was about four thirty, and Wes took the T to Government Center Station, which was one block from the meal. When he exited the station and crossed the street, he was shocked to see a line of people snaking around the building. He found out it was the line for the prerace meal. He took his place in line and hoped it would move fast because he needed to get off his feet.

The wait went by quickly. A man and his wife behind him started up a conversation with him, which helped pass the time. They were from California, and it was their first time in Boston. They were headed back to Monterey, California, to run in the Big Sur Marathon the following weekend.

"That's crazy," Wes told them. "I hope I'll be able to walk again by next weekend."

The line moved quickly, and Wes soon found himself under the covered entrance to the building where the buffet lines were set up. There was vegetarian pasta, pasta with meat, and chicken alfredo pasta with mixed vegetables. After loading his plate with vegetarian pasta and mixed veggies, Wes headed inside and found a spot to watch the highlights from the previous year's race. He quickly cleaned his plate and headed back for seconds. Other runners joined him at his table, but they were so engulfed in their own conversation that they barely noticed Wes.

The excitement in the air was almost palpable as the runners laughed and exchanged war stories from their marathon experiences. Wes tried to soak up as much as he could. He was in no hurry for the next twenty-four hours to pass. He silently thanked God for the experience and how truly blessed he was. Tears pooled in his eyes as he thought back to where he was twelve months earlier. *Thank you, thank you, thank you.* More runners were searching for places to sit.

Better get out of here.

Wes threw away his plate and picked up a goody bag of snacks and sweets as he exited. The volunteers wished him good luck as he left. At the hotel, he told Roxie about his excellent adventure. It felt good to hear her voice and know how excited she was for him.

"We'll be watching on TV tomorrow. Good luck!" she said. "Remember, you are a Warrior!"

After saying good-bye, Wes took a nice hot shower and headed to bed. He was like a kid on Christmas Eve. He closed his eyes, went through his mental checklist for the morning, and drifted off into a deep sleep.

He awoke with a start, thinking he was late for the race. Jumping out of bed, he was in full panic mode, trying to gather his senses for a second. As he stood up in the dark, he looked at the clock again and realized it was only five. He had been dreaming that he had overslept. He laughed at himself, settled under the covers, and tried to go back to sleep.

CHAPTER 25

HOPKINTON

Marathon morning finally arrived, dawning cloudy and chilly with temperatures barely reaching forty degrees. Having not been able to go back to sleep after his dream, Wes had been awake close to an hour before he finally got up at six. At least it was only a dream, and he had not really overslept. He had gotten about seven hours sleep, which was not bad for the night before a race. But it was all good. He was so excited he could hardly contain himself. Christmas was finally here!

Wes rushed downstairs to the complimentary breakfast at the hotel and gobbled down his standard prerace meal of two bagels, a banana, and some oatmeal. Since his corral didn't start until ten thirty, he knew he better eat extra to hold him over. He scooted upstairs, went to the bathroom quickly, jumped in his clothes, and caught the hotel shuttle to the T station at Alewife. He knew he had to get off at the Park Street Station, but he nervously double-checked his map after he took a seat on the subway just to be sure. When they stopped in Cambridge, about forty more runners got on. Wes remembered he wasn't the only one running that day, and he probably just needed to follow the crowd.

After four more stops, they arrived at Park Street. The subway was overflowing with extremely excited runners. Looking around, he felt a little lonely and thought what fun it would be to run with a group of friends. *Joy is always sweeter when experienced with others,* he thought. When the doors opened at the Park Street Station, the throng pushed up the stairs and onto Boston Commons. He could not believe the rows and rows of runners lined up on Boylston Street on the edge of the Commons to board the shuttle buses to Hopkinton.

Wow! What a crowd.

Thinking the lines might be shorter farther down the sidewalk, he began to walk down the street before finally picking one out. He stopped to look around, and it began to sink in. *It's finally here. I'm really running in the Boston Marathon.* Wes thought about how far he had come and all he had been through to reach that point in his life. He tapped his chest, pointed skyward, and silently thanked God. A tear came to his eye as he thought about Preacher.

This one is for you, buddy. He touched Preacher's cross that always hung from his neck.

Wes looked around at all the brightly colored runners. Some wore running shirts representing running clubs. Some were representing charities such as Team in Training and Dana Farber. Wes couldn't help feeling a little out of place with his yellow Wes's Warriors shirt and Clemson hat, but it was important to him that his kids see him with their shirt on in his pictures. And since he had forgotten to bring a throwaway long-sleeved shirt for the start, he had resorted to the old trash-bag warm-up jacket. Thankfully, he spotted several other runners wearing trash bags too.

After about ten minutes, they started boarding the bus. Wes couldn't help noticing how many family members were there to see their runners off. They seemed to be pretty emotional as they said their good-byes. Wes took a seat toward the back next to a guy from Iowa who was running Boston for the first time too.

They exchanged small talk about their running experiences and preparation for the marathon.

They soon began the forty-five-minute drive out to the start line. Bus after bus quickly pulled out and got on the Massachusetts Turnpike. Wes noticed the rocky terrain that appeared after they left downtown Boston. Boulders of all sizes were everywhere, and he was surprised by how much woodland there was. The terrain quickly changed from city row houses to open wooded areas. Near the Massachusetts Telephone & Telegraph Building, he noticed the biggest hawk he had ever seen. It looked so majestic in an old oak tree. Across the street, he saw several crows.

Not today, he thought. The thirty-mile drive went quickly as the buses evidently had been given the green light to get the runners out there as quickly as possible. They finally took the exit to Hopkinton. As they approached the prerace staging area at Hopkinton High School, Wes was surprised by how small the town seemed. The streets leading to the high school were narrow, and he wondered how all the buses were going to get in and out of there.

They eventually pulled up beside the high school gym. There was a big horseshoe-shaped banner that proclaimed, "Welcome to Hopkinton: The Start of the Boston Marathon!"

Several race photographers were snapping pictures.

Why not? Wes posed for his picture. After passing through the banner, he walked around to the back of the school. It opened up to the fields where there were tents with bagels, water, and carb gels for the runners. Runners were everywhere—stretched out on the ground wherever there was a small space and relaxing before their epic run. It looked like a big mosaic rainbow.

By now it was almost eight, and he had about two hours before his corral started. Runners are grouped together in corrals by their qualifying time, so that runners of the same pace run together. The elite women start first, thirty minutes before the elite men, so that the men and women winners cross at about the same time. Due to his fast qualifying time, Wes would be in the very first corral after the elites.

He found a spot to stretch out and rest. As he relaxed, his mind began to drift. He thought about his grandmother's words that God had a good plan for him, Preacher's New Testament teachings on the grace of God, and all the people who had chipped in to get him there. The feeling that bubbled to the surface more than anything else was an overwhelming sense of gratitude. He was grateful to be there and experience the great race, but he was mostly full of gratitude for his second chance at life. He began to pray quietly.

Dear God, I just thank you so much for loving me and giving me a second chance. Please help me make the most of this day and bring honor to Your holy name. Thank you, thank you, thank you.

With that thought enveloping him like a warm blanket, he drifted off to sleep.

Wes had been asleep about thirty minutes when he was awoken by the stirrings of other runners around him. He panicked for a second until he looked at his watch and realized he still had an hour. He got up, started stretching, and began going through his prerace warm-up routine. After about twenty minutes, he made a pit stop at one of the hundreds of port-a-lets in front of the school. He fell in with the huge, slow-moving crowd of runners making the half-mile journey toward Hopkinton's Main Street and the start line. There was laughter and excitement all around.

I wish I could bottle all this energy. I could make a lot of money with it.

A middle-aged man noticed Wes's Clemson hat and said, "Go Tigers! You from South Carolina?"

"Yes, sir. Greenwood. And you?"

"Yeah, lower part of the state, near Charleston. My name is Ernie, and this is my daughter, Evie."

Wes nodded to Evie and said, "Hi. My name is Wes."

"Wonderful day, isn't it?" Ernie asked.

"Best ever," Wes replied.

"First time?" Ernie asked.

"Yes, sir," Wes answered. "How about you guys?"

"This is our third time together—and my fifth," Ernie said.

"Wow. That's great. Congratulations."

"You are in for a real treat," Ernie said. "This is without a doubt the greatest marathon in the world, and most definitely the greatest sports fans in the world. All the towns along the way really come out and support the race. There will probably be close to a million people lining the route. All of them cheering and offering high fives. The Wellesley girls at mile thirteen are so loud and such a lift. And just wait till you get closer to downtown Boston near the Harvard and Boston College students. It will be so loud that you won't be able to hear yourself think, which at that point may be a good thing. It's so much fun. I like to run this one for fun and enjoy it—not kill myself. It's not like I'm going to place in my age group. This is the best of the best runners from all over. It's like a big all-star race of runners from around the world. I bet every one of them has placed in their age group or better at one time or another in a race. I'm just Joe Runner, and I'm so blessed to be able to qualify for it and get to run with all these elite folks. It's like the World Series, Super Bowl, and Final Four all rolled into one for me. And when that gun goes off, anyone could win. I know I won't, but a young buck like you might. Stranger things have happened."

They both laughed.

"Absolutely." Wes nodded in agreement.

Ernie laughed and pointed to a magnolia tree. "Let me tell you what I saw right up here at this magnolia tree the second time I ran here several years ago. Back then, they didn't have all these barricades up along the street to keep you out of people's yards, so people were sliding off peeing in flower beds and beside houses. Well, you see how that magnolia tree's branches go all the way to the ground? This guy went in there to pee, and, as soon as he got in there, we heard yelling and he came running back out with a cop right on his tail. Funniest thing you ever saw. The policeman evidently was hiding in there waiting for someone to try it."

Wes laughed and said, "Thanks for the warning."

They got to the start just in time to hear the National Anthem and see the military jets do their flyover. Wes couldn't help but notice that Ernie was quietly crying. Ernie shook his head and softly said, "It just really means a lot to me."

Wes patted him on the back and nodded.

They stood together for a few more minutes, taking in the scene. That narrow area of downtown Hopkinton had a few shops and houses enclosing it. The corrals were squeezed into Main Street and proceeded back for several hundred yards turning down Church Street.

"Well, I guess I better get in my corral," Wes said. "Enjoyed talking to you guys. Best of luck," he said as he shook their hands.

"Yes, best of luck to you too, Wes. See you at the finish line," Ernie replied.

"See ya," Evie said and waved as they parted company.

Wes moved into his corral just a few yards from the blue and yellow BAA unicorn emblem on the start line that had been painted there every year for more than twenty years by Jacques LeDuc.

The elite men had been gone for about twenty minutes, and there was nothing but open street in front of them beyond the start line. Wes looked around at the other runners in his corral and noticed how fit and competitive they looked.

I don't stand a chance in this group. I guess we'll find out if all that hill work pays off. He couldn't help but laugh. *If you told me a couple of years ago that I would be standing right here today, I would have said you were crazy. Thank you, Jesus.* He touched his chest and pointed skywards.

"Two minutes to start," came the announcement.

Game time, Wes thought.

In front of him, thousands of fans cheered. Behind him, thousands of runners from all over the world were chasing the dream of a lifetime for marathoners: competing in the Boston Marathon. Wes felt goose bumps tingle his skin as he looked over and watched the race official raise the starter's gun. He leaned forward in his starting stance.

With a bang, they were off.

CHAPTER 26

THE RUN OF A LIFETIME

Miles 1–6
Hopkinton to Ashland to Framingham

J ust past the start in the sleepy New England community of
Hopkinton is the steepest downhill of the course. The first mile
drops 130 feet—the equivalent of a thirteen-story building. The
throngs of runners and the narrow road will help slow a too-fast
descent. The course soon settles into rolling hills as you pass the
raucous party at TJ's Food and Spirits at mile 2. Midway through
mile 3 is the huge clock tower at the intersection of Union and
Chestnut Streets on the approach to Ashland. The course begins
to level out as Framingham waits at mile 5.

Wes said a quick thank you prayer, pointed upward, and took
off with the lead pack. After a thirty-yard flat stretch of road, the
course began to drop sharply down on a narrow stretch packed
with screaming fans. The sound was deafening to Wes and gave
him a quick jolt of energy. He was thankful to be at the front of
the tsunami of runners behind him. Between the approaching
downhill, the throng of runners pushing him from behind, and
his adrenaline, Wes had to resist the urge to turn on the jets. He

knew from his research that his quads would pay later if he made that mistake now.

Wes had never seen such a crowd of fans at a race before and a lively crowd at that. The cheers were deafening in the first half mile, but nothing compared to what he would hear ahead. He had to laugh when he heard a fan yell that they were almost there.

Easy for him to say, Wes thought.

A guy in a Santa suit was waving to all the runners. Wes waved back and smiled.

The enthusiastic crowd was not showing any signs of thinning over the first several miles. Wes wondered if it would be like that the whole way or just at the start. As he entered the small town of Ashland, he saw businesses on each side of the street. One in particular on the left caught his eye. It was a big wooden building with a big wooden deck filled with loud, cheering drunken fans. The sign said TJ's Food and Spirits. He couldn't help but wonder if they had been at it all night or just gotten an early start.

Wes was running with a pack of about a dozen other runners with no one ahead of them. *Interesting,* he thought. He took a quick inventory of how he felt—breathing was not labored, legs felt fine—and decided to stay with them for the time being. It was going to be a long run, so there was no need to sprint ahead and risk burning out later. He knew they were moving at a pretty good pace, and the clock confirmed that at the mile 2 marker. They had covered the first two miles in a little over eleven minutes.

Right on target—5:30 per mile. I can't believe I'm actually running in the Boston Marathon. Wow. This is so great.

He was grinning from ear to ear. He couldn't help but smile at this blessing he had been given—beautiful day, historic course, health, new lease on life. And the fans—the fans were four and five people deep along the entire course so far. They were clapping and cheering as hard as they could. What a lift that gave the runners. It was as if the cheers were lifting them up and pushing them toward downtown Boston; it was almost like they were surfing on a huge wave of love.

Wes didn't realize that the course actually went through eight small, picturesque Northeastern cities. As soon as they left one city, they were on the outskirts of another. That made it easy for the fans from each town to come out and line the course as the runners passed by. As much as possible, he tried to take it all in. He couldn't believe how rocky the terrain was on the sides of the road here too. Not gravel but big boulders. A lot of the houses and buildings were made of granite, which made the towns beautiful and distinctive. A very different landscape than he was familiar with in South Carolina.

As they approached Framingham, they encountered a decent half-mile climb. The pack showed no signs of slowing its pace as they lugged uphill. Wes noticed a building supply store with a big banner: "Congratulations, runners. Run strong."

Wes laughed and imagined it reading, "Run, Wes Strong!" Some of the fans were holding signs for specific runners.

Just past Framingham, Wes noticed a brick, two-story building. It was long and narrow with tall windows. A big arching window separated two second-story dormer windows. As they passed this neat old building, Wes realized it was the Framingham Train Station. He would read later that a train crossed the tracks there in 1907, stopping the lead pack and causing a major inconvenience. The pack Wes was in had to be careful not to trip as they crossed the tracks that cut across the highway. The course flattened out there, and the runners had to resist the urge to push the pace. Wes knew from his reading and from Coach Joe not to push it there.

Miles 7–12
Framingham to Natick to Wellesley

The next town on the course at mile 7 is Natick. The course begins to roll again with minor uphills after the runners pass the West Natick Train Station. At mile 9, the course flattens as Lake Cochituate appears on the right. Just past the lake is an historic district filled with quaint Victorian homes. Mile 10 leads through Natick Center, past the fire department and municipal buildings. The First Congregational Church with its tall steeple will be on the left. The course begins to climb uphill at mile 11, but after the first quarter mile, it rolls downhill until almost the twelve-mile mark. Thick woods appear on the right as the course temporarily becomes quieter.

As they entered Natick, the crowds began to swell in size. People were now ten to twelve deep on both sides of the road and very loud. Wes had to smile as he saw kids of all sizes and ages holding their hands out for high fives. There were even moms holding the hands of small infants out to join in the fun. The cutest though were the two- and three-year-olds trying to hold their hands up high enough to reach the runners. They would let out a squeal if they were successful in their endeavor. Some of them were so tired from holding their hands high that they had to use their other hand to support it.

And it wasn't just kids. Adults of all ages were yelling and high-fiving. Wes couldn't help but smile at this wonderful support. *No wonder they say New Englanders are the best sports fans in the world. If they do this for the marathon, I can only imagine what it is like for the bigger sports—football, baseball, basketball, and hockey.* He couldn't ignore all the outstretched hands, and when the course turned here and there, Wes drifted to the edge to cut the corner and high-five a few of the fans.

It was like he was feeding off their energy. All the yells of encouragement and the high fives seemed to be making him stronger. He was not tiring at all and felt very good. He had always felt like hilly courses were his strength. He assumed it was from all his cross-country training and hill sprints. Maybe Roxie was right; this course might suit him well. He sure hoped it was true.

They passed the West Natick Train Station on their left, and the crowds showed no signs of thinning. Wes was impressed that the locals had their own water stations set up for the runners in addition to the official water stations at every mile. And the amenities the locals offered were impressive. Some held out cookies. Some had orange slices. What was really thoughtful was that about thirty yards past the orange slices, someone would be holding out wet wipes for the runners to wipe their sticky hands and faces. His personal favorite was the fans giving away freeze pops. *Oh man. I haven't had one of those in forever*, he thought as he sped by. *Maybe next time.*

As they left Natick, the course continued to roll, but there were no major hills. Wes noticed several of their pack had fallen off the pace. They were down to seven or eight in his pack, and their pace was holding steady at 5:30 per mile. The fans appeared to thin, and trees appeared on both sides. A lake on the right and train tracks on the left offered little shoulder for fans. A man in a yellow kayak on the water waved to the runners. Wes returned his welcome.

After they passed the lake, the crowds picked up again as they entered Natick Center's lovely residential area. *This would be a neat place to come back and explore*, he thought. *Such a beautiful place.*

A distinctive red brick church on his left had a tall steeple rising above the thunderous crowds. They left Natick behind, and the course began to climb for a short distance. Soon, they were rolling downhill for almost a mile. The downhill was nice and appreciated. Suddenly, it got quieter as if something challenging loomed ahead. He was about to experience one of the trademarks of the Boston Marathon that can only be experienced in person. Words cannot describe the girls of Wellesley College.

Miles 13–19
Wellesley to Newton

Wellesley College suddenly appears on the right, but it's heard before it's seen. The course remains relatively flat through downtown Wellesley as the halfway point soon arrives. The next couple of miles offer more of the same before the challenges arrive. Mile 15 starts with a little climb before the course suddenly plunges downhill into lower Newton Falls where the mile ends. The course flattens as it enters Newton before starting a series of climbs that are not individually too tough, but the cumulative effect is challenging after already running almost sixteen miles. Over the next nine miles, the course is either dropping or climbing. Mile 16 includes one of the toughest hills on the course—noted more for its half-mile length than its steepness. The hills continue through miles 17 and 18 as the course passes though yet another residential area with huge crowds.

Wes was alone in his thoughts for a few minutes when he suddenly began to hear a roar in the approaching distance. The roar was continuous and sustained in magnitude—like when someone hits a home run. Wes wondered if something had happened ahead or if someone famous was passing through. It continued to get louder as the pack approached. Wes soon saw what looked like tall school buildings looming on the right, and as they came around a small bend in the road, the source of the uproar suddenly became evident.

Girls were packed in a tight screaming gauntlet on the right side of the road. They were leaning over the temporary railing and reaching out to the passing runners offering hugs and kisses. Some held hilarious posters offering kisses, marriage, and assorted other services. They were the girls of Wellesley College. Without a doubt the loudest, most excited, frenzied gathering of young females in one place at one time in the world stretching for almost a mile. Wes had completely forgotten about them, but he was sure to never forget them again. He had never seen anything like it. He had overheard one guy on the bus warning the other runners not to get too close because they would grab you and try to pull your clothes off. With that in mind, Wes kept a safe distance and high-fived a few of them, but he couldn't help but smile at the whole spectacle.

That definitely gave the pack a boost, and they soon entered downtown Wellesley and the halfway point. The crowds were huge and loud there too. They were now closer to Boston than Hopkinton, and the real race was about to begin. The next mile continued relatively flat—"the calm before the approaching storm"—Wes had read. Wellesley was another charming residential area with beautiful stone buildings. They continued their steady pace, and as Wes looked around, he thought they might have dropped another runner. He took a quick systems check and feeling good, he began to look strangely forward to the next nine miles to see how he would fare. Would he be up to the challenge? Would his extra training pay off?

Mile 15 started with a little climb, and as they crested it, they could see a sudden plunge of about a hundred feet that bottomed out in Newton Lower Falls. They soon entered Newton proper and began to climb a pretty tough hill. It was not that steep, but it was more than a half mile long.

Here we go, Wes thought as the pack continued to maintain its pace.

They crossed over a highway on an exposed overpass that Wes thought could be very difficult on windy days. Thank goodness that was not the case this day. Wes noticed a hospital on the right—Newton Wellesley Hospital—as they crested the hill.

The course flattened temporarily at mile 17, and they made a fairly sharp turn at a firehouse. There was another huge crowd there, and a band on the back of a flatbed truck was playing "Sweet Home Alabama."

That song seems a little out of place in Boston, Wes thought, but the effort was much appreciated. They next hill was steeper than the last but not as long. After cresting it, Wes's pack was down to four runners.

Those two hills must have gotten a couple of them, Wes thought.

Mile 18 continued relatively flat or slightly downhill. Wes and his pack continued to maintain their pace and used that section to recover a little before the *big* challenge looming ahead. Wes was glad he had done his research on the course and knew what to expect. It would be easy to go out too fast on this course and then crash and burn on the tough hills that waited after the midway point. Not that he had made it yet.

Wes noticed Newton City Hall at mile 19 and remembered a famous statue for the legendary Johnny Kelley, who was twice a winner here and sixty-one times a finisher. The "Forever Young" statue depicts a young Kelley running alongside an elder Kelley. Wes glanced around to both sides of the road, but could not see a statue. He turned his attention back to the course, which was soon rising uphill again. It was another short but steep one that Wes and his pack soon crested.

Which one of these is Heartbreak Hill? Oh yeah. Not yet. Not yet.

Miles 20–24
Newton to Brookline

The steep half-mile known as Heartbreak Hill waits ahead as the course crosses the twenty-mile mark. It's not the longest or steepest hill most runners will see in their careers, but placed at mile 20 after several other grueling hills makes its name appropriate. The ample crowds lining it provide a much-needed psychological boost. At mile 21, the course enters the Boston College area with its screaming students and begins to descend mercifully for a half mile. The course passes a cemetery at mile 22 as the course levels out for a short half-mile stretch through Cleveland Circle before a short climb into Brookline. Descending along Beacon Street through Brookline's Washington Square neighborhood, the course mostly descends as it parallels the Green Line trolley tracks with restaurants and shops on both sides. Coolidge Corner will appear along mile 23 with its distinctive Tudor-style business building on the left. A glimpse ahead in the distance will reveal the most iconic feature of the Boston Marathon—the huge Citgo sign to the left of the course that signals one mile to go.

Wes soon enough found himself entering a wide stretch of residential area that angled steeply uphill for half of a mile. He couldn't see the top, but he knew that this was it—Heartbreak Hill—the graveyard of Boston Marathon dreams of glory. It was so named because in 1936 defending champion John A. Kelley caught up with the race leader, Ellison "Tarzan" Brown, here and gave him a pat on the shoulder as he passed him. This gesture evidently gave Brown the motivation he needed as he went on to win the race in front of Kelley. A local journalist said the outcome of this act "broke Kelley's heart." Wes wondered which of the two runners he would be today. He decided he would be "Tarzan" Brown and continued to maintain his pace. He put his head down, shortened his stride, and pumped his arms, letting the crowd help lift him up the hill with their roar. Little did he know they were cheering for him alone as he was slowly pulling away from the pack step by step, stride by stride.

When Wes crested this icon of the running world, he wanted to stop and shout that he had made it up Heartbreak Hill. Saner thoughts prevailed however, and he quickly caught his breath on the run and pushed onward. Listening to the deafening roar of the fans, he took a short glance around and realized there were no other runners with him. Taking a few more strides, he took a longer look back and saw the next runner ten yards or more behind him.

Wes was shocked to suddenly find himself alone at the front of the first wave of runners. This was not unwanted—just totally unexpected. He knew they had pushed the pace, but he never thought he would be leading the wave at that point. Wes was in a conundrum. Should he slow and run with the pack or risk upping his pace, and potentially tiring, to see what he could possibly do? Up to that point he had just been happy to be there floating alone on a wave of fan-induced endorphins and enjoying the experience. But he felt pretty good, and he knew the worst of the hills were behind him.

This internal debate was playing out in his head as he scooted up another short incline and caught a glimpse of the big scoreboard at mile 21. It was showing the winning male cross the line. Wes did not see the winner's name, but he did see his time of 2:15 even.

Wow, that's pretty fast, Wes thought. His current time was 1:48. Up to that point, he had not really had a time goal. He had wanted to stay around 5:30 per mile as long as he could and hopefully break two hours and thirty minutes. He suddenly realized he was ahead of that pace, and if he really pushed it, he might get very close to the elite winner's time. He also knew it was way too early to start daydreaming about glory.

As the debate raged on in his head, he started thinking of Preacher and the guys in McCormick. Distance running does a funny thing to the mind. It's as if once the body is brought into submission by the miles, the mind is free to go places— deep pure places. In Wes's younger days, it was usually dark, punishing places, but the new Wes knew better. He felt Preacher with him. He could hear his last words to run for him and the other Jesus Freaks in the McMarriott. He could hear him telling him that God had big plans for him. He suddenly was oblivious to the screaming Boston College fans along the next mile. He had a mission. Wes didn't know why God had placed him in that position, but he knew he had to do his very best and see what God had in store.

Wes made up his mind to push really hard for the last 4.5 miles. Sensing his effort, the crowds got louder and louder as he approached. The course began to flatten out and then gradually descend as it entered Cleveland Circle. Dodging the trolley tracks crossing the course, Wes decided to really use this downhill and began to pump his arms faster and faster in an effort to gain speed. It was not a race to beat his competitors or obtain a certain time; it had suddenly become about giving his very best for his Lord, Preacher, and all the inmates struggling to overcome their pasts. He was beginning to labor under the effort, but he continued to push onward like a man on a mission.

The course paralleled the Green Line trolley tracks as it entered Coolidge Corner along mile 23. Descending gradually after a short uphill, Wes continued to push hard. He didn't know if he could keep this sprint up for three more miles, but he was going to give it everything he had. Glancing up, he saw the second favorite site to the runners, besides the finish line. Rising above the buildings in the distance was the huge iconic Citgo sign that signaled one mile to the finish line. Wes had read that the sign was the most recognized sign in the world to marathon runners. All he could muster was a faint smile and a prayerful thank you to the heavens as he continued to push on.

Miles 24–26.2
Brookline to Boston

A half-mile downhill enters Brookline as the course passes through a sea of restaurants and stone condo buildings on each side of the road. It undulates slightly through this mile until at the top of a slight hill awaits the glorious Citgo sign at mile 25. This hill passes over the Massachusetts Turnpike and drops slightly as Fenway Park appears on the right. Kenmore Square is next with its thunderous crowds. Dropping down slightly into an underpass below Massachusetts Avenue, the course quickly rises up into a screaming tunnel of fans as it turns right onto Hereford Avenue before a sharp left onto Boylston Street. Two hundred yards ahead is the most magnificent sight in all of marathon racing: the bright blue and yellow finish line of the Boston Marathon.

***

Back at the Bowers-Rodgers Home where Roxie had decided to go to watch the race before starting her shift, she and the morning moms were gathered around the television in the den as they watched the toddlers on the floor and rocked the infants. They had just finished lunch and were trying to get the little ones to sleep so they could see if they could catch a glimpse of Wes.

With one eye on the kids and one on the television, their attention was torn between the two until the announcer said, "Frank, we have a developing story out on the course. There seems to be a non-elite runner from the first wave who could possibly challenge the winning time. Now we've seen this in other years, and they usually fade in the last miles after Heartbreak Hill, but this runner is actually lowering his pace. We don't have his name yet, but we should know shortly."

Roxie glanced at the TV and did a sudden double take. Jumping to her feet and running toward the set, she immediately recognized Wes's bright yellow Warrior shirt. She let out a squeal. "It's Wes. It's Wes. Quick, go get Joan. I don't believe it. He's running his tail off. Go, Wes, go!" What had been a lazy, quiet afternoon at the home suddenly became a fever pitch of activity as everyone gathered around and began to cheer frantically as if Wes could hear.

Joan flew in the room and said, "What in the world is happening?"

Roxie said, "Look! It's Wes. He's leading all the runners. Well, all the runners except the elites. Look at him go!"

"You're kidding!" Joan exclaimed. "That's wonderful. How much farther does he have to go to the finish?"

"About two miles," Roxie said.

They all gathered closer to watch.

***

Wes continued to give it his all. He had to dig deeper than he ever had in a race. He didn't know why or what it would mean, but he knew he had to keep pushing. He just kept thinking about Preacher and all he had done for him: how he protected him in prison, how he befriended him, and how he died for him. Preacher had kept preaching the gospel to him until Wes was finally ready to receive Christ into his life. He kept picturing Preacher's dying face and hearing his last words. He desperately wanted to make him proud. It was as if he were right there running with him.

Wes thought about his friends back in McCormick and what this might mean to them. He knew what any kind of encouragement could do for their psyches. Just to see a fellow inmate accomplish something good on the outside. And how could he forget everyone at Bowers-Rodgers and how they had taken him in like family. Joan had taken a big gamble on him, and he wanted to bring some positive attention to the home. He thought about the kids he had worked with. How proud would they be to wear their Warrior shirts if he did really well? And he thought of Roxie. He had no idea what she saw in him or why she kept encouraging him to run. How could she know that good was going to continue to come from him running? She meant so much to him—and he did not want to let her down.

Most of all, he thought of his relationship with Christ. He was so thankful to have that now, and he truly believed that good could come out of every situation as Romans 8:28 says. He had not figured out why so much bad happens, but he was determined to keep his faith no matter what—in all situations good or bad. Like Preacher had said, "Just keep looking forward and making deposits in that faith bank, and you will get good returns!"

Wes became oblivious to the roar around him, looked ahead and up to the heavens, and prayed for strength.

***

Back in Greenwood, everyone stood around Roxie in front of the television set. The infants were all asleep, and the women were holding hands as if in a prayer circle to will Wes across the line.

The announcers said, "Frank, we have confirmation on the name of that lead runner in the first wave. His name is Wes Strong from Greenwood, South Carolina. We know he ran for

Clemson a few years back and this is his first Boston, but other than that, we don't know anything about him. Other than the fact that he is turning in an unbelievable finish. If he continues on this pace, he will be very close to the winning time. This is truly unprecedented. Now he would not be eligible for the prize money as the elites have already crossed the line, but boy what a story it would be!"

The women of Bowers-Rodgers cheered frantically for their young hero.

"Go, Wes, go!"

"Hang in there, Wes!"

"You can do it!"

***

On the course, Wes had just passed the glorious Citgo sign, but he barely noticed. His thoughts were erratic. Most of the oxygen was being shunted to his cyanotic, aching legs. His thoughts bounced from Preacher to the kids to Roxie. Most of all, he prayed for the strength to finish strong and somehow bring glory to God. Wes had never sprinted so hard on such dead legs, and he was really worried that he might collapse at any moment.

Lord, please don't let me fall down.

Wes went over an overpass with a short incline that was a leg zapper at this point and dropped down under the Massachusetts Avenue underpass. The roar of the fans had been constant for several miles, and he had been lost in his thoughts. Wes was totally unprepared for what hit him as he emerged from the tunnel. Word had spread back through the crowd that an American amateur had a chance to beat the winning time. As he emerged into the sunlight, a deafening roar nearly knocked him off his feet.

"Go, Wes, go!"

It was just the jolt of adrenaline he needed for the final stretch.

As he turned onto the short stretch of Hereford Street, the crowd was in a total frenzy. American flags were waving as the fans packed every inch of sidewalk to get a glimpse of this new wonder kid. The echo of his name coming off the city buildings was unexpected and moving.

Tears streamed down his face as Wes made the turn alone onto Boylston Street. A kaleidoscope of pictures of all those who had believed in him flashed through his mind: Preacher, Joan, Roxie. He pumped his arms with all he had left in a last-ditch effort to maintain speed.

***

Roxie was jumping up and down, and all the other women were screaming for pure joy as the announcer said, "Here he comes. He's really got a shot. It's going to be close. Oh boy. I can't believe what I am seeing."

***

Wes tried to focus through his tears, and just two hundred yards ahead, he could see the glorious bright blue and yellow finish line.

Just a little more. Just a little more.

With every step, it got a little closer, and then he caught sight of the official time clock to the right of the finish line. It was on 2:14. He knew he had to be under 2:15, so he closed his eyes for the last twenty yards and gave it everything he had. He opened them just in time to catch one last glimpse of the clock before he crossed the line. He was afraid he was hallucinating, but it was still on 2:14:50 something. He had done it!

As soon as he crossed the line, he collapsed and grasped his hands in prayer. "Thank you, God! Thank you! All the glory is to You!" He looked up long enough to touch his heart with his right hand and point upward to the beautiful cloudless sky before falling onto his back.

Pandemonium hit everywhere simultaneously.

The television announcers screamed, "He did it! He did it!"

The fans on Boylston roared their approval, and the women of Bowers-Rodgers back in Greenwood were ecstatic. Tears flowed freely at both sites at this joyous, totally shocking occurrence. Who would have thought it was possible?

When the race officials reached the spent, prostrate body of Wes Strong on Boylston Street, he was sobbing uncontrollably. His arms were crossed over his face, and his emotions flowed freely. His chest heaved, trying to get oxygen to his aching legs.

The officials asked if he was okay.

Wes opened his eyes when he heard a Middle Eastern accent saying, "Wes, my friend, it is good to see you. How are you?"

Wes attempted to focus his blurry eyes, but he could not make out the face that went with that somehow familiar voice. As he lifted his shoulders off the asphalt in an effort to sit up, several hands reached out and helped him stand. As he reached his feet, his legs wobbled.

The officials supported him to keep him from falling.

A dark-skinned, smiling face said, "Wes, my friend, that was a very good race. Very good indeed!"

"Abdi?" Wes replied when he recognized the voice. It was Abdi Montohan from high school. The same Abdi that Wes had kept from falling in the state finals that allowed Abdi to win. The same Abdi that had gone on to run for the University of Oregon and was now running professionally, unbeknownst to Wes until that moment. What a surprise! For a second, Wes was afraid the lack of oxygen had damaged his brain.

"Yes, my friend, it is me. It is my turn to help you up. Here, I give this to you." Abdi smiled and held out the laurel wreath worn by every Boston Marathon winner. "But I will keep the check," he said with a laugh.

"You won?" Wes asked.

"Yes. Yes, I did." Abdi grabbed Wes's hand and lifted it in a joint sign of victory as the throng of spectators at the finish roared their approval.

Cameras flashed all around at the wonderful spectacle.

A reporter thrust a microphone forward and said, "Wes, this is incredible. What do you have to say?"

Wes looked down, took a deep breath, and gathered his thoughts. "I just want to thank God for this. All the glory is His. I am just so thankful, so grateful."

Another reported asked, "What club do you run for in South Carolina? Who are the Warriors on your shirt?"

Wes replied, "I don't run for a club. I work at a children's shelter in Greenwood, South Carolina, called the Bowers-Rodgers Home, and this is the Warriors for Christ shirt we give our kids who run with me. And, by the way, we are in sore need of donations if anyone would like to help."

"Abdi, how do you two know each other?" another reporter asked.

Abdi laughed and told the story about the state championship. "So, I look forward to racing my old friend again," he said with a laugh. "Good day. This is a very good day."

"Yes, it is," Wes said as he and Abdi embraced again.

The BAA officials allowed Wes a massage and other amenities in the elite runner's area. Before they gave him a ride back to his hotel after more interviews, Wes asked if he could possibly use a telephone.

***

Back at the Bowers-Rodgers Home, the ladies were trying to get the babies back to sleep.

When the phone rang, Susan answered it and heard a familiar voice say, "Hey Susan. It's Wes."

"Wes!" she screamed. "Wes, we're so proud of you. Roxie, come here quick! It's Wes!"

Roxie sprinted to the phone and exclaimed, "Wes, I don't believe it! How did you do that?"

"I can't believe it either," Wes said. "Romans 8:28 is all I can say."

"Well, that's exactly right. Joan said the phones have been ringing off the hook in the office with people wanting to donate money since they saw you on TV. That is so wonderful!"

"Wow," Wes replied. "That's great. I'll call you when I get back to the hotel, but I just wanted to call and thank you for believing in me. I love you, Roxie."

"I love you too," Roxie replied.

CHAPTER 26.2

ROMANS 8:28

If there was one thing life had taught Wes, it was that there was not a "before and after." There is not a "before prison" and an "after prison" or a "before my mom or dad died" and an "after my mom or dad died." Or a "before Boston" and an "after Boston." Or a "before this choice" and an "after this choice." There is only yesterday and now.

Yesterday is gone. It cannot be changed, and it does not have to affect the present. Let it go. There is only now. We only have control over now and the next decision we make. Pray for God's guidance in every decision—large or small. Try to do His will in the next decision facing you, and move forward in His good and perfect will for you. Live for now and do the best you can, letting the Holy Spirit be your guide. If you make a mistake, admit it to God and ask for the wisdom to learn from it. And move on.

This had been the message Wes had learned from Preacher, and he found it to be true in all his Christian readings. This was the message he was trying to share in his prison ministry and with the kids at Bowers-Rodgers. It was who he had become, and he was not about to let his success in Boston change his mission. If anything, he hoped it might give him a broader platform from which to share it.

215

Wes was living Romans 8:28, and he shared that every chance he got during the interviews in the days after Boston. He was absolutely determined to not let his celebrity go to his head; instead, he would use it to share the gospel. He had suddenly been given a bigger audience, and—with sincere gratitude in his heart—his greatest desire was to share Preacher's message. His death would not be in vain.

As one would expect, Wes was deluged with requests for interviews in the days after Boston. Several of the major networks interviewed him in Boston before he left the next afternoon. Then, in the days after returning to Greenwood, Channel 4 from Greenville and Channel 7 from Spartanburg came to town to talk to him. *The Index Journal* had a big spread on him. In all of these, he stuck to his mission—giving God the glory, speaking of Romans 8:28, and the work that he, Roxie, and the other staff members were doing at Bowers-Rodgers. Wes did his best to divert the attention from himself and onto what God can do in a surrendered life. He didn't know how long his moment of fame would last, and he did his best to make the most of it in the proper way.

The Saturday after Wes returned from Boston, he went to McCormick to see his friends and show them his finisher's medal. What a celebration that was! Even the warden turned out for that visit. Wes learned that the guys had been allowed to go into the lunchroom to watch the race, and they saw him finish. They were all so excited and proud that one of their own had made good on the outside.

"Yo, Wes," Watts teased. "Can I have your autograph?"

"Get out of here, Watts," Wes teased in return. "Seriously, guys, I just wanted to make you guys proud and let you see things can work out okay. Like Preacher always said, 'All it takes is faith and trust.'"

"To Preacher," Wolf said.

"To Preacher," they all replied.

Things slowly began to get back to normal in Greenwood, except that whenever Wes went for a run, people would recognize his bright yellow Warrior shirt and wave or honk at him. He had to laugh though when he received notification from the BAA that his picture had been chosen as the only picture from the marathon to be in Boston photographer Ellen Proctor's yearly calendar. She had been positioned at mile 19—as always—and caught his picture pulling away from the pack. It became his favorite photo from the race.

Three weeks after the marathon, Wes was relaxing in the swing on his front porch after a short run.

The mailman hurriedly stopped his delivery truck in front of Wes's house.

"Hey, Steve," Wes called out.

"Wes, I'm sorry I haven't seen you since you got back. So proud of you, man. Congratulations," Steve said.

"Thanks," Wes replied.

"Hey, I've got a certified letter for you. I sure hope it's good news with those five colorful circles in the corner."

Taking the letter, Wes saw the familiar symbol of the United States Olympic Committee in the return address corner. He gave Steve a quick glance and ran inside to grab a pen to sign for it. He scribbled a signature and thanked Steve before going back inside. He quickly opened the letter and began to read the shocking news.

Dear Mr. Strong,

The United States Olympic Committee would like to congratulate you on your wonderful recent achievement at the Boston Marathon. In lieu of this and your significant work at the Bowers-Rodgers Home, and in an effort to field the strongest team possible for the upcoming Summer Olympics, we, the ruling body of the USA Olympic Committee, have made the unprecedented decision to waive the exclusion for convicted felons to allow you to participate in the US Olympic Marathon Trials to be held this year in November in New York City the day before the New York City Marathon.

Wes fell to his knees in front of his couch and sobbed. With his elbows on the couch and his hands clasped in prayer, he began to pray through his tears.

Dear God in heaven. Thank you. Thank you. Thank you for your glorious blessings. Thank you for the second chance you have given me, and please help me to continue to use it to glorify you. Thank you, most of all, for your Son Jesus Christ, in whose name I pray. Amen

Wes moved to the couch and reread the letter over and over again. Nodding slowly in confirmation as the tears rolled down his cheeks, he softly repeated the words of Romans 8:28. "We know in all things God works for the good of those who love him and are called according to his purpose."

Donations to the Bowers-Rodgers Home can be sent to:

Bowers-Rodgers Home for Abused Children
PO Box 1252
Greenwood, SC 29648